157
O23c

CONTEMPORARY THEOLOGY
AND PSYCHOTHERAPY

CONTEMPORARY THEOLOGY
and
PSYCHOTHERAPY

by

Thomas C. Oden

THE WESTMINSTER PRESS

PHILADELPHIA

LIBRARY OF CONGRESS CATALOG CARD NO. 67–11798

PUBLISHED BY THE WESTMINSTER PRESS®
PHILADELPHIA, PENNSYLVANIA

PRINTED IN THE UNITED STATES OF AMERICA

To My Wife, Edrita

Contents

Introduction

It is ironic that at a time when the parish minister and the practicing psychiatrist seem to be on the most cordial terms in recent times, the theological disciplines seem increasingly withdrawn from hardheaded dialogue with the exciting new dimensions in psychiatry and psychotherapy. If the immediate postwar period witnessed a spate of discussions by some of our best theological minds [1] on the potential rapprochement of psychology and theology, their efforts have borne meager fruit in this present decade with recent literature tending increasingly toward trivia and repetition.[2] In fact, some of the more interesting and imaginative recent theological interpretations of psychology have been coming from nontheologians Norman O. Brown, Erik Erikson, O. Hobart Mowrer, and Abraham Maslow.[3]

This once-lively dialogue seems to have been abandoned, unfortunately, at a time when contemporary theology was ripening for a mature theological interpretation of the process of secularization (Gogarten, Bultmann, Bonhoeffer, Braun, Vahanian) [4] and the action of God in universal history (Pannenberg, Congar, Ogden, Moltmann).[5] Thus the regrettable gap between pastoral care and current theology is growing at a time when it should be narrowing. While students of pastoral care have felt increasingly mystified by the somewhat esoteric hermeneutical and historical issues with which contemporary theology is at present preoccupied, theologians have neglected the increasing involvement of the church's ministry in healing relationships and the remarkable new developments in the behavioral sciences which might impinge meaningfully upon our discussions of hermeneutics, secularization, and authenticity. With the passing of Tillich, it is now difficult to name a single major voice in systematic theology that seems committed resolutely to pursuing the dialogue with psychotherapy. In Europe only Köberle has remained in the fray,[6] and in America the last major contribution from a systematic theologian was by Daniel Day Williams in 1961.[7] As a whole, the theological disciplines have seemed content to leave the dialogue in the hands of those whose essential interests and professional commitments were practical and operational rather than systematic or exegetical. This disengagement might be conveniently blamed upon the introverted attitude of professional specialization in Continental and especially German theology, which admittedly hangs as a millstone around the neck of all serious interdisciplinary dialogue, were it not for the fact that it is equally acute in American theology with a long interdisciplinary tradition to support it.

All this is especially deplorable at a time when psychotherapeutic theory and practice are undergoing such vast, rapid, diverse, and dramatic changes that make outmoded many of the issues that were being hotly discussed only ten years ago. At an astonishing pace there are new developments and discoveries in social psychology, group psychotherapy, anthropological medicine, ego and identity psychology, transactional analysis, learning theory, the biochemistry of illness, and new developments in medications for the treatment of mental illness, and continued proliferation and interaction among diverse schools of behaviorism, psychoanalysis, client-centered therapy, and existential phenomenology. Already strong polemical currents may be found within recent psychotherapeutic literature, and constructive correctives have been undertaken by influential psychologists, *against* the very inadequacies in earlier psychotherapy about which theologians used to complain, so that now the older issues must be radically reframed.[8] The apparent abandonment of the dialogue by theologians is further to be regretted at the precise time when certain types of psychotherapy (notably existential psychiatry and the group therapy movement) seem to be openly looking toward the resources of the Christian tradition, if not for guidance at least for partnership and conversation on the interpretation of man and the healing process.

In such a context this effort can only be a rudimentary attempt to refocus the conversation in terms of certain new theological initiatives which seem to hold promise for the proper maturing of the now retarded dialogue. Although it is beyond the purview of this inquiry to attempt to summarize these current developments in clinical practice and therapeutic theory, I do intend to clarify how certain new initiatives in theology have potential (although as yet quite unexplicit) relevance for the emergent forms of psychotherapy. I have chosen a single theological theme, Christ's worldly formation, as delineated by two major recent theological thinkers, Bonhoeffer and Teilhard, to help us refocus the issue and illustrate some potential new lines of inquiry.

If education is risk (in the sense that one must risk taking a position in order to learn whether one is right), then this discussion is surely a part of the author's own education. For it is offered not as a finished position but as a direction of potential inquiry, not as a program but as an attempted clarification of an undeniable theological intuition, with the expectation that it will be criticized and improved by its critics.

If some may be puzzled that this study on psychotherapy and pastoral care is undertaken by one whose basic training is in theological ethics, they may note that we have good precedent in the Christian tradition from Justin Martyr to Bonhoeffer that demonstrates that ethics and pastoral care (or moral and pastoral theology) stand in an intimate and inseparable relationship. Recent fragmentation of university disciplines into introverted enclaves of expertise, and of theological fields into carefully protected jurisdictions of specialization, has done incalculable damage to the study of man. If in many faculties of theology there still exists a notable but often unmentionable split between the study of the " practical disciplines " (in which pastoral care is usually included) and the study of systematic, Biblical, and historical theology, the time is surely overdue for theology to reclaim pastoral care as an intimate concern without which its work becomes increasingly irrelevant and abstract, and for pastoral care to reclaim its older and exalted position as a focal dimension of the total task of theology. The thrust of this essay is strongly directed toward an interdisciplinary approach to the interpretation of the healing process, which is witnessed to by the fact that it was written during a year of study at the Psychiatrische und Neurologische Klinik of Heidelberg University, which took the author far afield from theology proper into an intensive study of psychotherapy.[9]

In *Kerygma and Counseling*, I have defended the proposal that there is an *implicit* ontological assumption hidden in all effective psychotherapy which is made *explicit* in the Christian proclamation, and that by means of the analogy of faith the process of psychotherapy may be understood as an arena of God's self-disclosure. Now I ask: What are the implications of this thesis for theology in an era of rapid secularization, and for psychotherapy in a time when theology is grasping a deeper perception of the worldliness of the Word of God?

PART ONE

NEW INITIATIVES

A theological interpretation of the secularization process is the most decisive issue in contemporary Protestant and Catholic theology. The very shape of the church in the next generation may hinge upon how we answer this question.

Two thinkers in particular, Bonhoeffer and Teilhard, have taken significant initiatives to reformulate radically our questions on a theology of the saeculum (the world, this present age). Taken together, they represent the profoundest contribution of Protestant and Catholic thought toward a potential reframing of the issues between contemporary theology and psychotherapy.

CHAPTER I

A Theology of the Saeculum

Although Dietrich Bonhoeffer's thought on religionless Christianity continues to have an explosive impact upon secularizing Protestantism, little effort has been made to relate it concretely to secular academic disciplines. Ironically Bonhoeffer has been read and appreciated chiefly by religious people, however much his theology protests against *homo religiosus*. The unfinished task of those who share Bonhoeffer's unfulfilled concerns is now to engage him in a conversation with those for whom religion is mostly a thing of the past. We shall limit our discussion to the promise of Bonhoeffer's theology for one specific major life-option of our time: psychotherapy, an area in which his contribution may have as much relevance as it has already had in the areas of ethics, ecclesiology, and lay renewal.

Although most students of the biography of Dietrich Bonhoeffer know that he was the son of a well-known authority on psychotherapy and neurology, a leading professor of psychiatry at the University of Berlin, and that Dietrich's childhood was spent in a setting thoroughly familiar with Freudian psychoanalysis and the psychotherapies of the first two decades of this century, little or no attempt has been made to ask about the martyred theologian's own view of the healing process or the possible relevance of his theological program for psychotherapy. It is curious that in *Die mündige Welt*,[1] the four volumes of essays assessing Bonhoeffer's work, none of his interpreters so much as

mention his relevance for pastoral care or secular psychotherapy.[2]

Yet for many of us the issues between current theology
and psychotherapy remain mostly muddled and unre-
solved. Frankly, as I deliberately reexamined the witness
of contemporary theology hopefully for some fresh, illuminating word for this conversation, the results were disappointing, until the insight suddenly dawned recently
that virtually everything Bonhoeffer was saying about the
"matured world," the concreteness of Christ's formation
in the world and worldly Christianity, offers a penetrating
new clue for pursuing this somewhat stagnated dialogue.
Although admittedly Bonhoeffer has said very little directly about the therapeutic process as such, his whole
style of thinking, his basic *modus vivendi* as theologian,
may give us the possibility of grappling with the issue in
a radically different way.

Bonhoeffer's *Ethics* is the most decisive point at which
we can begin an engagement of his thought with our
theme. Returning from America to Germany in 1939 to
continue his leadership of the makeshift, illegal, Gestapo-
hunted seminary at Koslin, Bonhoeffer began to work on
a startlingly new approach to ethics which he viewed as a
long-term project. On April 5, 1943, Bonhoeffer was ar-
rested for conspiring against the Hitler regime. From
Tegel prison, however, he continued to nurture these new
lines of thinking, now collected in *Prisoner for God*. In
1944, after the failure of the plot to kill Hitler, Pastor Bonhoeffer was removed to a Gestapo prison in Berlin, later
to Buchenwald as a special prisoner, and subsequently,
after a brief court-martial, was hanged in the concentra-
tion camp of Flossenburg, April 9, 1945, only a few days
before that area was reached by the American Army.[3] All
his theological reflections during the war years, therefore,
remain unfulfilled by sustained systematic clarification,
and must be read as unfinished, and often embryonic theological intuitions.

1. THINKING IN TERMS OF TWO SPHERES

Bonhoeffer has described the symptoms of a theological disease that we believe has infected virtually all attempts to engage theology in dialogue with psychotherapy. He calls it "*thinking in terms of two spheres.*"[4] From better to worse examples of this dialogue by participants of widely varying hue — from Allport to Asmussen, from Thurneysen to Tournier, from Goldbrunner to Sheen[5] — none seems to have escaped this mind-set of thinking in terms of two spheres.

To think in terms of two spheres means to divide reality up into two antithetical categories: sacred/secular, divine/worldly, revelation/reason, grace/nature. The pernicious danger Bonhoeffer sees in this is that the action of God is reduced to a partial matter, a part of reality amid other realities, instead of participating in reality as a whole. All "two sphere" thinking imagines that there are realities which lie outside the reality that is in Christ. Thinking in terms of two spheres would suppose, for example, that the process of psychotherapy might be perceived as lying outside the reality of grace.

The trouble with such thinking is that it creates "the possibility of existing in a single one of these spheres, a spiritual existence which has no part in secular existence, and a secular existence which can claim autonomy for itself."[6] The prototypes of such bifurcated thinking are the *monastic* withdrawal, which protects the sacred from the secular, and the *secularist* reductionism of the nineteenth century, which guards the autonomy of the secular against religious and metaphysical pretensions. Against both of these Bonhoeffer protests: "So long as Christ and the world are conceived as two opposing and mutually repellent spheres, man will be left in the following dilemma: he abandons reality as a whole, and places himself in one or the other of the two spheres."[7]

Accordingly, the problem in our encounter with psychotherapy is to break the spell of "thinking in terms of two spheres," a habit as chronic among secularists (Freud, Fromm, e.g.) [8] as it is among religionists (Bergsten, Olsen).[9] This pattern of thinking is just as persistent among psychological proponents of religion (Allport, Jung, Mowrer) [10] as it is among religious proponents of psychology (Stern, Dicks, Johnson).[11] But according to another perception of the Christian witness, " There are not two realities, but only one reality, and that is the reality of God, which has become manifest in Christ in the reality of the world." [12] To deal with reality is to deal with that reality which has been dealt with by God in Jesus Christ. To perceive it as anything less than reconciled is to perceive it inadequately. Reality means: that which God perceives, knows, judges, creates, and redeems. All concepts of reality that do not take into account God's own dealing with the world are, in Bonhoeffer's view, abstractions. " The reality of God discloses itself only by setting me entirely in the reality of the world, and when I encounter the reality of the world it is always already sustained, accepted, and reconciled in the reality of God." Therefore one can never experience " the reality of God without the reality of the world or the reality of the world without the reality of God." [13]

As we deal with psychotherapy and the kerygma, we do not confront two spheres standing side by side, competing with each other, attacking each other's frontiers. (" If that were so, this frontier dispute would always be the decisive problem of history.") No, we cannot pursue the dialogue on any other assumption than that " the world, the natural, the profane and reason are now all taken up into God from the outset." [14]

But if such worldly realities as psychotherapy are already circumscribed by grace, what becomes of the church and its pastoral care? Does the church have any " territory " to call its own in the healing process? " The space of the Church is not there in order to try to deprive the world of a piece of its territory, but precisely in order to prove to the world that it is still the world, the world which is loved by God and reconciled with Him. The Church has neither the wish nor the obligation to extend her space to cover the space of the world. She asks for no more space than she needs for the purpose of serving the world by bearing witness to Jesus Christ and to the reconciliation of the world with God through Him." [15] Applying this to the therapeutic process, one might say that the church is not trying to take over the therapist's secular function or extend her space over the therapeutic process. The church does have a legitimate space within the world, but only that which is fitting for her unique service and witness, to point the world to the reality in which it already stands!

Accordingly the central theme of Bonhoeffer's *Ethics* is: " Whoever sees Jesus Christ does indeed see God and the world in one. He can henceforward no longer see God without the world or the world without God." [16] Consequently Bonhoeffer proposes: " It is now essential to the real concept of the secular that it shall always be seen in the movement of being accepted and becoming accepted by God in Christ." Genuine secularity is thus defended and affirmed by authentic Christian proclamation, for " there is no real possibility of being a Christian outside the reality of the world and . . . there is no real worldly existence outside the reality of Jesus Christ." [17]

This unique perception of secularity now leads us directly toward the central issue of our essay: How does psychotherapy as a humanistic process participate in and embody the reality of Jesus Christ, and how does Christ take form in and through this unique interpersonal relationship? The heart of our answer is that effective psychotherapy mediates and embodies the unconditional acceptance and understanding love present in being itself, which Christian proclamation announces as a once-for-all event in Jesus Christ. Without this mediation and embodiment, psychotherapy simply does not work. [18]

But why should we choose psychotherapy, with all its ambiguities, as a special test case for the validity of Bonhoeffer's theological project? Because therapy continues to offer dramatic examples of how our society through ostensibly humanistic means has learned to help broken people into wholeness, overcoming many forms of guilt, anxiety, and meaninglessness which once were thought to have only a religious solution. Here we encounter a living tradition of secular ministry in which depression is being undercut by human self-understanding, neurotic guilt being transformed into self-acceptance, anxiety into openness, and (to use the dramaturgic language of the Bible) the demons are being overthrown! In that sense psychotherapy represents something of a problem, even an embarrassment, to religiosity, and when it is most profoundly effective, it becomes the most profoundly embarrassing. For, to put it crassly, if it is actually possible for humanistic, agnostic therapists to do all this, what are we religionists left to do? To whom do we appeal in jurisdictional disputes over who cures what ailments?

Bultmann in his exchange with Heidegger settles the jurisdictional dispute in an interesting way. Admittedly, he says, Heidegger can speak of the formal possibility of authentic existence, but he cannot make this an actual, realizable (ontic) possibility for a particular person. Without the Christ event one may describe authenticity and health, but to conceptualize health is quite different from actualizing it.[19] Although we have affirmed this distinction, it is clear that Bultmann's boundary with Heidegger does not apply meaningfully to psychotherapists who do not only talk about the formal ontological possibility of authentic human existence, but actually go about the process of realizing authenticity in persons to a recognizable degree, not merely describing but mediating to the troubled person a relationship in which he can grow toward congruence, health, self-acceptance, and reconciliation with himself and the world.

2. Reframing the Jurisdictional Dispute

Bonhoeffer's theology of secularization helps us to reframe the issue precisely at the point where Bultmann's boundary is inadequate for psychotherapy. For if indeed God and the world are one in Christ, and if to know the world is to know its participation in Jesus Christ and to know Jesus Christ is to know his concrete formation in the world, then the whole boundary dispute must be reconceived. The clues to Bonhoeffer's transformation of the question may be found in the following concepts: (*a*) unconscious Christianity, (*b*) the emancipation of worldly processes, (*c*) the natural, (*d*) formation, and (*e*) relative autonomy.

a. In his letter from prison of July 27, 1944, he speaks of "*unconscious Christianity*" as "a subject with which I am more and more concerned." [20] Repeatedly he draws upon a distinction made in older Lutheran dogmatic thought on infant baptism, in which there is a kind of direct, unconscious faith (*fides directa*), which makes the Sacrament efficacious. It is not a deliberate, reflective, conscious faith (*fides reflexa*) but a faith directly given to the child and mediated through the *sanctorum communio*. So he proposes an arresting analogy between faith in infant baptism and the presence of an "unconscious faith" among men who do not realize it, which "may never be captured by reflexion," [21] but which nonetheless "rests on the objectivity of the event of revelation." [22] Such a *fides directa*, we suggest, may from time to time appear in the therapeutic process without recognizing itself as such. However absent may be the *fides reflexa* (the conscious and reflective response of man to the Word of God in Christ) in the profane language of therapeutic conversation, one may nevertheless be open to Christ's taking form in himself to move toward authenticity.

b. What Bonhoeffer as theologian most fervently hopes for worldly processes is merely that they be *"emancipated for true worldliness,"* i.e., "for the state to be a state," or in our case, for psychotherapy to *be* psychotherapy. "The primary implication for secular institutions of the dominion of Christ . . . is not, therefore, the conversion of the statesman or the economist," [23] or the therapist, in an individual sense, but instead the maintaining and enhancing of their genuine worldliness. The goal is not to "Christianize" the state, economy, or the healing process, but instead to help them function toward their proper ends of justice, production, and health.[24] "The purpose and aim of the dominion of Christ is not to make the worldly order godly or to subordinate it to the Church but to set it free for true worldliness." [25]

In a truly perceptive conclusion to his essay on "' Personal' and 'Real' Ethos," Bonhoeffer says: "When the Church perceives that a worldly order is on some few occasions possible without the preaching being heard (but still never without the existence of Jesus Christ), this will not impel her to disregard Christ, but it will elicit from her the full proclamation of the grace of the dominion of Christ. The unknown God will now be preached as the God who is known because He is revealed." [26] Thus, if the therapeutic process is able to nurture authentic human existence even *without* the church's proclamation being heard, this does not mean that Jesus Christ is not at the center of things (here as always), but that he is taking shape in the world without that Word being consciously heard and understood, and that there is no reason for the church to be embarrassed by the presence of the Holy Spirit apart from the church, or for the theologian to rush to the therapist and tell him he cannot accomplish this healing without Christ! Instead, such processes will elicit from the church grateful acknowledgment of the grace of Christ in the midst of worldly relationships, and wherever her preaching is able to be heard, she will say that the

God who is hidden in the world has made himself known in Jesus Christ.

c. Bonhoeffer was distressed that Protestant thought had almost entirely abandoned the concept of " *the natural* " to Catholic ethics. He felt that this was a substantial loss which deprived Protestant thinking of a framework for dealing with secularity. If grace is so misunderstood as to make nature unimportant, a costly blind spot results in Protestant fideism. While basically affirming Barth's critique of natural theology, Bonhoeffer nevertheless wanted to recover the concept of the natural, but to do so on the new basis of a Christological exegesis of reality. So with uncommon originality, he defined the natural as " the form of life preserved by God for the fallen world and directed towards justification, redemption and renewal through Christ." [27]

Mark carefully his penetrating distinction between unnatural (twisted, neurotic) and natural (that which moves toward health and full functioning): " The natural is that which, after the Fall, is directed towards the coming of Christ. The unnatural is that which, after the Fall, closes its doors against the coming of Christ. There is indeed only a relative difference between that which is directed towards Christ and that which closes its doors to Christ." [28] Although difficult to grasp, this distinction is decisive. It means that both the natural and the unnatural are defined *relative* to Christ. While the natural moves toward health, fulfillment, and the embodiment of divine love, the self-destructive forces of neurotic guilt, repression, and psychosis can finally do no more than move against the stream of the natural, and define themselves only in their opposition to the embodiment of divine love.

Readers familiar with the tradition of psychotherapy from Horney to Maslow,[29] which powerfully relies upon health-giving forces within man's own natural self-actualizing tendency, may find an unexpected companion in Bonhoeffer, who, amid the unnatural terrors of the Nazi regime while he himself was being hunted by the Gestapo, wrote: "It is in the last analysis life itself that tends towards the natural and keeps turning against the unnatural and bringing about its downfall. This, in the last analysis, is what underlies the maintenance and recovery of physical and mental health. Life is its own physician, whether it be the life of an individual or the life of a community; it wards off the unnatural because the unnatural is a destroyer of life; only when life itself is no longer able to offer the necessary resistance do the destructive forces of the unnatural carry off the victory." [30] Psychotic withdrawal heralds just such an unnatural victory. The therapeutic process works with the natural and thus toward the concrete formation of divine love in human behavior.

Anyone who has seriously considered Carl Rogers' therapy, which doggedly relies upon the natural resources of the self for therapeutic growth, is struck by his persistent, stubborn, almost incredible faith in the strength of the natural to fight against neurosis and move the self toward authenticity, provided one is given a safe context for self-exploration. [31] In a theology of revelation so consistent as Bonhoeffer's, however, one is amazed to find a firm corroboration for just such a genuinely naturalistic optimism: "In this context there is a solid basis for that optimistic view of human history which confines itself within the limits of the fallen world. . . . We are referring here to an entirely immanent optimism, one which is entirely rooted in the natural." [32] In this connection Bonhoeffer notes with appreciation the view of psychiatrist Fritz Künkel, for whom "life" is always the "final corrective of what is psychically unnatural and diseased." [33]

d. Perhaps the most crucial Bonhoefferian construct which calls for a reformulation of the jurisdictional issue, however, is that of *concrete formation*. His ethics is essentially an ethics of formation, i.e., of Christ taking form in us. The formation of which the New Testament speaks is not our forming of ourselves, or formulating plans, programs, or policies to shape the world, but instead God's own love taking shape concretely in our midst, becoming embodied in interpersonal relationships, assuming living form in the flesh. Such formation is not a product of our initiative but takes shape in our willing response to God's initiative. "We cannot transform ourselves into His image, it is rather the form of Christ which seeks to be formed in us (Gal. 4:19), and to be manifested in us." [34]

Although Bonhoeffer himself never was able to explore the rich implications of this ethic, we suggest that the therapeutic process may witness powerfully (although always ambiguously) to just such a worldly formation of Christ's love. For what takes place in effective psychotherapy is a reforming of human self-understanding in response to the reality of acceptance mediated through the human brother, a process which we believe already has an implicit theological assumption. Bonhoeffer himself was at least clear that Christ's worldly formation directs man ever anew toward his authentic humanity. "To be conformed with the Incarnate — that is to be a real man. . . . To be conformed with the Incarnate is to have the right to be the man one really is. Now there is no more pretence, no more hypocrisy, or self-violence, no more compulsion to be something other, better and more ideal than what one is. God loves the real man. God became a real man." [35] If therapy, despite its limitations, succeeds in helping direct man toward his own true humanity, if it too loves the real man amid all his self-defeating illusions about himself, if it too struggles against the compulsion to be something other than one is, then in some sense it is a partner and a partaker in Christ's worldly formation.

While the church remains the essential locus of Christ's taking form in history, it points constantly away from itself and toward Christ's concrete formation in the world. For " the concept of formation acquires its significance, indirectly, for all mankind only if what takes place in the Church does in truth take place for all men." Accordingly, "the Church can be called the Body of Christ because in Christ's Body man is really taken up by Him, and so too, therefore, are all mankind. . . . What takes place in her takes place as an example and substitute for all men." All this assumes a unique and simple definition of the church: "The Church is nothing but a section of humanity in which Christ has really taken form." [36] Is psychotherapy thus a hidden form of the church? No, because it lacks the overt proclamation of the Word and celebration of the Sacraments which point explicitly to the accepting reality upon which therapy relies.[37] It is at best an ambiguous embodiment of true humanity. It is not a malformation, but an often healthy formation that lacks only the capacity to celebrate the one who is giving it shape.

e. Although he warned against it's being misinterpreted, Bonhoeffer spoke of a "relative autonomy," or perhaps more descriptively, a Christocentrically interpreted autonomy, for secular processes. To speak of the formation of Christ amid secular processes such as psychotherapy does not mean that they are made subject to an alien rule, for "he came unto his own," and "by him all things consist." [38] For it is precisely the Lordship of Christ that most profoundly wishes for these secular processes that they "attain to their own true character and become subject to their own innate law." This cannot mean that they are left to be governed by what Bonhoeffer calls "the arbitrary rule of a so-called 'autonomy' which is fundamentally nothing but lawlessness, *anomia*," but that "under the dominion of Christ they receive their own law and their own liberty." [39] Psychotherapy, as a case in point, must be invited by theology to function in terms of its own self-directed way of operation without constant theological intrusion, although it is not in the last sense fully interpretable from within its own limited framework.[40]

When reality is bifurcated, however, and the world is viewed as if it owned its existence apart from God, the result is a spurious "love of the world" against which the

New Testament inveighs, a phony worldliness that simply fails to love the world as God loves it. Bonhoeffer thus warns against a destructive " love for the world which is enmity toward God (James 4:4) because it springs from the nature of the world as such and not from the love of God for the world. The world ' as such ' is the world as it understands itself, the world which resists the reality of the love of God which is bestowed upon it in Jesus Christ." Although the world, on behalf of its own spurious autonomy, struggles against the church, " it is the task and the essential character of the Church that she shall impart to precisely this world its reconciliation with God and that she shall open its eyes to the reality of the love of God, against which it is blindly raging." [41]

Are we therefore implying that the life of faith is achievable through secular means without the Christian proclamation? However true it may be that certain forms of authenticity and health are realized in effective psychotherapy, Christian koinonia knows that this kind of ambiguous, fragmented, " unconscious Christianity," or natural proto-authenticity, has a right to experience a deeper understanding of its own inner reality, viz., the incarnation, the word of God which takes shape in us. Christ's coming is that point in history where we have been freed to know fully that we are indeed accepted by God himself — not merely by our therapist or ourselves — and that the future is guaranteed by the God who has made himself known as trustworthy.

CHAPTER II

Bonhoeffer's Theology
and Religionless Psychotherapy

From April 5, 1943, to April 9, 1945, Bonhoeffer was imprisoned. The ideas that emerged from his prison cell have become so very influential in Protestant theology that, in addition to Barth and Bultmann, Dietrich Bonhoeffer has become the leading spokesman of a whole new school of "worldly theology." It was especially during the summer of 1944 that his thinking on religionless Christianity, in which he set forth a constellation of embryonic theological proposals that have penetrating relevance for our dialogue with therapy, emerged with real force.

1. THE WORLD COME OF AGE

If one were to identify the pivotal events in theology during the past generation, in addition to Bultmann's programmatic essay and Pope John's call for an ecumenical council, one might also speak of the probing letter that Bonhoeffer wrote to Eberhard Bethge on April 30, 1944, from Tegel prison: "You would be surprised and perhaps disturbed if you knew how my ideas on theology are taking shape. . . . The thing that keeps coming back to me is, . . . We are proceeding towards a time of no religion at all: men as they are now simply cannot be religious any more. . . . Our whole nineteen-hundred-year-old Christian preaching and theology rests upon the 'religious premise' of man . . . but . . . the linchpin is removed from the whole structure of our Christianity to date." He then asks what might result " if we had finally to put

down the western pattern of Christianity as a mere pre-
liminary stage to doing without religion altogether. . . .
How can Christ become the Lord even of those with no
religion? " [1]

The question is further elaborated: " What is the significance of a Church . . . in a religionless world? How do
we speak of God without religion, i.e., without the tem-
porally-influenced presuppositions of metaphysics, inward-
ness, and so on? How do we speak . . . in a secular fashion of God? In what way are we in a religionless and secular sense Christian, in what way are we the *ekklesia*, ' those
who are called forth,' not conceiving of ourselves religiously as specially favoured, but as wholly belonging to
the world? Then Christ is no longer an object of religion, but something quite different, indeed and in truth
the Lord of the world." Later he wrote: " Let me briefly
summarize what I am concerned about: it is how we
can reclaim for Christ a world which has *come of
age*." [2]

His letter of May 25, 1944, which wrestled with the interaction of science and Christian faith, directly speaks to
our discussion with psychotherapy: " It is possible nowa-
days to find answers to these problems which leave God
right out of the picture. It just isn't true to say that Christianity alone has the answers. In fact the Christian answers are no more conclusive or compelling than any of
the others. Once more, God cannot be used as a stop-gap.
We must not wait until we are at the end of our tether:
he must be found at the centre of life." [3] The movement
of history toward increasing autonomy since the thirteenth
century has " in our time reached a certain completion."
In psychology, politics, art, and ethics, man has discovered the laws by which he lives in the world and manages
his affairs. " Man has learned to cope with all questions of
importance without recourse to God as a working hypothesis. . . . It is becoming evident that everything gets along
without ' God,' and just as well as before. As in the scientific field, so in human affairs generally, what we call

' God ' is being more and more edged out of life, losing more and more ground." [4]

Is not this the setting of the present dialogue? Although Protestant theology has become increasingly indebted to the behavioral sciences for its interpretation of man, it has nonetheless yearned to cling to some "territory" that would remain the distinct preserve of religion. The boundary has had to be renegotiated repeatedly since the thirteenth century, and the territory for specifically religious questions has become smaller and smaller. Psychology, as a case in point, has become increasingly sure of itself, able to do quite well on its own without theism as a working hypothesis. Understandably, both Catholic and Protestant interpreters, with quiet alarm, have continued to view the secularizing process as defection from the truth.

A Christian apologetic has emerged, therefore, to try to prove to this world come of age that it needs religion, that it cannot do without it. Admittedly, many of these once sacred questions have been surrendered to a secular pluralism, but certain " ultimate issues " allegedly remain, like guilt and death, for which we continue to reserve specifically religious answers, although the square footage of this territory seems to be getting smaller with every generation. *But* what if one day even these " ultimate questions " should be taken over by secular hands and answered by our culture entirely without the God of theism? [5] Such is already the case in current psychotherapy, which is increasingly dealing with such questions as meaninglessness, guilt, idolatry, and death.

How does a theology that remembers the God of the Bible respond to such a challenge? Bonhoeffer's answer is: with utter honesty, repentance, and intellectual sincerity. " We have to live in the world *etsi deus non daretur*," [6] as if " God " (in the sense of a *deus ex machina*) were not there. But it can also rejoice that the secularizing process from Descartes to Freud, by which " God " has been pushed more and more out of a religious enclave in the world, has opened the way for an abandonment of a false conception of God and a "clearing of the decks for the God of the Bible." So it is in psychotherapy as in secularization generally that "our coming of age forces us to a true recognition of our situation *vis-à-vis* God." [7]

Precisely because the church has been defensively fighting this rearguard action for self-preservation as if guarding its territory were an end in itself, it has, time and again, missed its chance to speak to the modern world. Now we are in an ironic situation in which traditional language must "become powerless and remain silent, and our Christianity to-day will be confined to praying for and doing right by our fellow men. Christian thinking, speaking and organizing must be reborn out of this praying and action." Meanwhile, it may not be helpful to try to communicate with the troubled in therapy in terms of the traditional language of the church. Rather, we must learn to "make present" our proclamation of God's deed in a new, active, secularized language, a "non-religious interpretation of biblical concepts." There will come a day when we will again be able to utter the word of God, but it will be in "a new langage, which will horrify men, and yet overwhelm them by its power." Until then, the Christian cause may be "a silent and hidden affair." [8]

If religion, in Bonhoeffer's definition, means man's quest for God, then Christianity, which speaks essentially of God's quest for man, is not, in that sense, a religion. It is unfortunate, however, that the theologian who has most powerfully introduced the notion of religionless Christianity never had time to provide a clear and consistent definition of it. Although we might reasonably assume that Bonhoeffer has in mind Barth's definition of religion,[9] he never validates this assumption. Repeatedly, Bonhoeffer's prototypical image of religiosity is circumcision viewed as a condition for justification.[10] At one point, he suggests that religion in his definition means "to speak on the one hand metaphysically, and on the other hand, individualistically," and elsewhere, religion means variously "individualistic concern for personal salvation," "concern for the next world," reliance upon a *deus ex machina,* or using God as a " working hypothesis." [11]

It is clear, in any event, that Bonhoeffer's rejection of religion on behalf of Christian faith and obedience calls for a review of most of the attempts to bring psychology into dialogue with Christianity in the last fifty years, since the majority of these contributions have employed a generalized concept of religion that often fits snugly into Bonhoeffer's own astute descriptions. The almost endless maze of writings on " psychology and religion " from the pens of Fromm, Guntrip, Biddle, Allport, McKenzie, *et al.,*[12] often tend uncritically to presuppose a concept of religion that any post-Bonhoefferian theology will find unacceptable. Although certain psychotherapies may have much in common with religion in general, this does not mean that they therefore have an ally in the Christian proclamation about the God who loves us not because of but in spite of all our religious pretensions, and grasps us amid our attempts to assign him a useful role as a human problem solver.

Religion of the sort Bonhoeffer protests must be rejected not only by Christian faith but also by psychotherapy. Of course, it is already being rejected by most current therapies that require no *deus ex machina* to bail them out at crucial times. Let us then pursue the dialogue between therapy and theology on the assumption that we are discussing the relationship between a religionless psychotherapy and a religionless Christianity, and see where this takes us. This, at least, appears more promising than the often abortive attempts of the religious psychologists, such as Allport or Jung, or the psychological religionists, such as Tillich or McKenzie.

2. THE REVOLT FROM BELOW

In a discussion which proposes that Bonhoeffer has profound relevance for our dialogue with psychotherapy, it is admittedly a bit of a handicap that Bonhoeffer himself had such harsh and biting words against the forms of psychotherapy that he knew, and, in fact, said almost nothing encouraging or affirmative about these possibilities for dialogue. It is clear, however, that the older forms of psychotherapy which he felt called upon to protest have now been surpassed by current psychotherapy. Thus, his polemic must be seen as altogether legitimate in an earlier behaviorist and Freudian setting but increasingly dated by the vigorous development of post-Freudian changes in psychotherapeutic practice. But we owe it to Bonhoeffer, nevertheless, to examine carefully just what he feared in "the revolt from below" and why he himself did not choose the psychotherapy he knew as a promising partner for Christian proclamation. It is necessary to allow him to speak, even if at length, in his own words:

We have of course the secularized off-shoots of Christian theology, the existentialist philosophers and the psychotherapists, who demonstrate to secure, contented, happy mankind that it is really unhappy and desperate, and merely unwilling to realize that it is in severe straits it knows nothing about, from which only they can rescue it. Wherever there is health, strength, security, simplicity, they spy luscious fruit to gnaw at or lay their pernicious eggs in. They make it their object first of all to drive men to inward despair, and then it is all theirs. This is secularized methodism.[13]

"Secularized methodism" is a term of utmost contempt for Bonhoeffer, for it signifies what is worst in Protestant pietism being taken over and "used" by psychotherapy in the world come of age, viz., a stratagem that convinces men they are in the worst possible predicament, only then to propose itself as the only solution. A certain brand of pastoral care has tended to follow at the heels of this secularized methodism of psychotherapy with an inclination toward

"priestly" snuffing around in the sins of men in order to catch them out. It is as though a beautiful house could only be known after a cobweb had been found in the furthermost corner of the cellar, or as though a good play could only be appreciated after one had seen how the actors behave off-stage.[14]

The emergence of psychotherapy in modern history is related to the world's "coming of age" in the following way:

When God was driven out of the world, and from the public side of human life, an attempt was made to retain him at least in the sphere of the " personal," the " inner life," the private life.[15]

Psychotherapy emerged as a scavenger upon the rotting flesh and bones of religiosity. Bonhoeffer continues:

The secrets known by a man's valet, that is, to put it crudely, the area of his intimate life — from prayer to his sexual life — have become the hunting ground of modern psychotherapists. In this way they resemble, though quite involuntarily, the dirtiest gutter journalists. Think of the newspapers which specialize in bringing to light the most intimate details about prominent people. They practice social, financial and political blackmail on their victims: the psychotherapists practice religious blackmail. Forgive me, but I cannot say less about them.

From the sociological point of view this is a revolution from below, a revolt of inferiority. Just as the vulgar mentality is never satisfied until it has seen some highly placed personage in his bathing attire, or in other compromising situations, so it is here. There is a kind of malicious satisfaction in knowing that everyone has his weaknesses and nakedness. In my contacts with the outcasts of society, its pariahs, I have often noticed how mistrust is the dominant motive in their judgements of other people. Every act of a person of high repute, be it never so altruistic, is suspected from the outset. Incidentally, I find such outcasts in all ranks of society. In a flower garden they grub around for the dung on which the flowers grow.[16]

This tendency to mistrust all motives and view every person as a patient (an attitude which, hopefully, current psychotherapy is beginning to outgrow) led Bonhoeffer to conclude that we should give up " our regarding of psychotherapy and existentialism as precursors of God. The importunity of these people is far too aristocratic for the Word of God to ally itself with them. The Word of God is far removed from this revolt of mistrust, this revolt from below. But it reigns." [17]

Bonhoeffer's intention was to protest against a premature alliance with a partner who persisted in dehumanizing man by viewing him only in his sickness. In this protest, ironically, Bonhoeffer himself fell victim to the same sort of mistrust against which he was protesting.[18] Despite his own intuitions, however, we remain convinced that his objections were directed against a now-obsolete style of therapy, and that his overall theological perspective is much more favorable to dialogue with the current situation in psychotherapy than he himself imagined possible.

It is astonishing, for example, how similar is Bonhoeffer's discussion of "correspondence with reality" and the psychotherapeutic view of "the fully functioning person," whom Rogers describes in these terms: "Experiencing has lost almost completely its structure-bound aspects and becomes process experiencing — that is, the situation is experienced and interpreted in its newness, not as the past." [19] In his brilliant essay on "The Fully Functioning Person," Rogers writes: "For the person who was fully open to his new experience, completely without defensiveness, each moment would be new. . . . Consequently such a person would realize that 'What I will be in the next moment, and what I will do, grows out of that moment and cannot be predicted in advance either by me or by others.'" [20] Similarly, Bonhoeffer says of the responsible, authentic man that "his conduct is not established in advance, once and for all, that is to say, as a matter of principle, but it arises with the given situation. He has no principle at his disposal which possesses absolute validity . . . but he sees in the given situation what is necessary and what is 'right' for him to grasp and to do." [21]

Note, further, how Bonhoeffer's language about God the healer corresponds with the empathetic function of the helper in therapy: "While we are distinguishing the pious from the ungodly, the good from the wicked, the noble from the mean, God makes no distinction at all in His love for the real man." If Protestant pietism has been overly busy distinguishing sheep and goats, effective psychotherapy has been making no such distinctions at all in its positive regard for the man as he is. Likewise, God himself does not allow Christian obedience to "classify men and the world according to our own standards and to set ourselves up as judges over them. He leads us *ad absurdum* by

Himself becoming a real man and a companion of sin-
ners . . . . God sides with the real man and with the real
world against all their accusers." [22] Similarly, effective
therapy leads the troubled person only in a unique way by
following him through his own expressions of inner conflict, sharing his situation as companion, entering his frame
of reference, siding with him in the form of understanding, regardless of who may be against him. It is often only
in the consciousness that someone is unconditionally with
him in understanding and for him in positive regard that
real healing takes place. [23]

In a unique distinction between ultimate and penultimate, Bonhoeffer affirms that in Protestant theology the
last word, the ultimate, is always justification of the sinner
by grace alone. The question of the penultimate, however,
has to do with the "things before this last thing," taking
with relative seriousness the human words before this last
divine word. Bonhoeffer asks whether this last word is always the most fitting word in every human relationship,
using an example that is of prime interest to our discussion: "When I am with someone who has suffered a bereavement, I often decide to adopt a 'penultimate' attitude, . . . remaining silent as a sign that I share in the
bereaved man's helplessness in the face of such a grievous
event, and not speaking the biblical words of comfort
which are, in fact, known to me and available to me." [24]
Sharing in the sense of limitation of the neighbor is a basic
element of the therapeutic process. The best way Bonhoeffer could signify this in bereavement was not by ver-
balizing about how the person is helpless, but by demon-
strating his sharing in his helplessness through *silence,*
which itself is a sort of helplessness in the form of language. Bonhoeffer then asks himself why, in this context,
he does not go ahead and witness to the ultimate. "Is it
from mistrust of the power of the ultimate word? Or is
there some good positive reason for such an attitude,
namely, that my knowledge of the word, my having it at
my finger-tips, in other words my being, so to speak, spir-

itually master of the situation, bears only the appearance of the ultimate, but is in reality itself something entirely penultimate? Does one not in some cases, by remaining deliberately in the penultimate, perhaps point all the more genuinely to the ultimate, which God will speak in His own time? " [25] The effective psychotherapist, likewise, refuses to impose upon the troubled person some kind of ultimate interpretation that would, in effect, falsify his empathetic participation in the radical limitation of the neighbor. That would simply demonstrate his own spurious "mastery" of the situation and more deeply his unwillingness to share seriously in the internal reality of the individual's conflict. Bonhoeffer suggests that such a "penultimate" attitude embraces the whole domain of the Christian life, but "especially the whole range of Christian pastoral activity." [26]

Only five days before the attempt to assassinate Hitler failed, Bonhoeffer proposed this strange formula: "The God who is with us is the God who forsakes us." [27] In this connection, he quotes Mark 15:34, Jesus' expression on the cross, "My God, my God, why hast thou forsaken me? " Likewise in therapy, it is the one who is for us, the empathetic therapist, who in a sense "*forsakes*" us, leaves us to ourselves, lets us radically choose ourselves without overweening guidance, permits us to be ourselves even amid anger, anxiety, and emptiness, and who thereby allows us to discover our own humanity. "God allows himself to be edged out of the world and on to the cross. God is weak and powerless in the world, and that is exactly the way, the only way, in which he can be with us and help us. Matthew 8:17 makes it crystal clear that it is not by his omnipotence that Christ helps us, but by his weakness and suffering." [28] Therapeutic help similarly emerges only after a certain sort of crucifixion, viz., the death of the therapist's own imperialistic desire to control the decisions of the other, the burial of his inclination to shape the destiny of others, based on the subtle assumption that he knows finally what is best for them. The therapist makes his best contribution to the health of the troubled man not through the strength of his opinions, judgments, calculations, or diagnoses, but in a sense through their absence, i.e., in and through a relationship with the neighbor in which he is freed to explore and discover his own present possibilities in his own language.[29] In a sense, the best therapy occurs when the client is most deeply alone, on his own, free to feel his own feelings.

3. THEOLOGICAL RESOURCES FOR THE EMERGING DIALOGUE

We conclude our discussion of Bonhoeffer's relevance to psychotherapy by reviewing his own assessment of the major voices in Protestant theology, asking how they are more or less adequate for the emerging conversation with therapy.

a. The strength of *theological liberalism* was that it accepted a lively relationship with the newly matured world and did not try to turn back the clock. In relation to psychotherapy, e.g., it ventured out (against more conservative protests) to learn (albeit uncritically) all it could about the psychological dynamics of sickness and health from the behavioral sciences. Its Achilles' heel, however, was that " it allowed the world the right to assign Christ his place in the world: in the dispute between Christ and the world it accepted the comparatively clement peace dictated by the world." [30] Of the legion of the earlier American discussions of religion and psychology, most have been caught in this process of accommodation and absorption.

b. Bonhoeffer's persistent quarrel with *Tillich* is his decisive use of the concept of religion. " Tillich set out to interpret the evolution of the world itself — against its will — in a religious sense, to give it its whole shape through religion. That was very courageous of him, but the world unseated him and went on by itself; he too sought to understand the world better than it understood itself, but it felt entirely *mis*understood, and rejected the imputation. (Of course the world does need to be understood better than it understands itself, but not ' religiously,' as the religious socialists desired.) " [31]

For Tillich, with his definition of religion as ultimate concern, psychotherapy becomes an arena in which religious concerns are expressed, just like art or philosophy. But for Bonhoeffer, with his definition of religion as man's outmoded, inauthentic quest for God, the worst possible category through which to interpret secularizing history is the notion of " religion."

Tillich's view that the Christian proclamation speaks primarily on the " boundary situation " of human existence is likewise challenged by Bonhoeffer, who says, " The Church stands not where human powers give out, on the borders, but in the center of the village." [32]

Against Tillich's principle of correlation, Bonhoeffer cuttingly writes: " It is necessary to free oneself from the way of thinking which sets out from human problems and which asks for solutions on this basis." [33] In a style reminiscent of Barth, Bonhoeffer condemns the method of correlation (allowing culture's questions to frame the questions for theology) on the grounds that Biblical theology strictly moves " not from the world to God but from God to the world," [34] and that the divine initiative must be just as decisive in framing the theological question as it is in speaking to its solution.

c. *Barth* was the first to direct a kerygmatic polemic against religion, showing how the protection of religion presupposed a failure to understand the kerygma. If attempts such as Tillich's were still " unintentionally sailing in the channel of liberal theology," Barth's decisive contribution, " his greatest service (the second edition of his *Epistle to the Romans,* in spite of all its neo-Kantian shavings)," [35] was his sharp distinction between religion and Christianity. Barth initiated the line of thought that viewed religion (man's quest for God) as directly opposed to Christianity (God's quest for man). But Barth did not finish what he started.

Barth's crippling inadequacy, in Bonhoeffer's view, has

been his " positivist doctrine of revelation," which does not
leave room for " non-religious interpretation of theological
concepts." So his contribution has tended to lapse into a
conservative "restoration" of the Calvinist-Augustinian
tradition.[36]

d. To Bonhoeffer, only *Bultmann* seemed to be aware of
Barth's limitations and tried to transcend them with his
proposal on demythologizing, a subject on which Bonhoeffer deeply reflected during his imprisonment. On May 9,
1944, he wrote: " My view of it today would be not that
he went too far, as most people seem to think, but that he
did not go far enough. It is not only mythological conceptions, such as the miracles, the ascension and the like
(which are not in principle separable from the conceptions of God, faith and so on) that are problematic, but
the ' religious ' conceptions themselves." [37]

Although these do not exhaust the alternatives in contemporary theology, they certainly cover some of the more
important ones. In our previous discussion, we have dealt
at length with Barth's potential contribution to the dialogue with therapy, and in subsequent chapters of this
study we shall make more detailed comments on the contributions of Tillich and Bultmann. But in general, we find
the astute observations of Bonhoeffer on the resources of
contemporary theology to be just as pertinent today as
they were when first written in 1944 and able to provide a
reliable vantage point from which to launch our discussion
of contemporary theology and psychotherapy.[38]

Although he never had an opportunity to pursue it himself, Bonhoeffer would undoubtedly have welcomed a
tough-minded dialogue between a theology of revelation
and the current vitalities of psychotherapy, which have
assumed so many priestly functions; but it would certainly
have been a living dialogue and not an innocuous monologue. It could never be a mere passive listening to the
therapists as if they were to lay down the rules of the game
or to assign a place for Christ in the processes of life.

4. THE BARTHIAN FOUNDATION

The careful reader may suspect that this book, with its Bonhoefferian-Teilhardian direction, represents a change of mind from the previously Barthianly oriented discussion of *Kerygma and Counseling*. Such is not the case, since the manuscripts for both books were in process together and, in fact, were earlier intended to be a single volume. Bonhoeffer's contribution is, furthermore, a direct and dependent consequent of the groundwork laid in the early volumes of Barth's *Dogmatik* and, in fact, anticipates much that finally appeared in its later volumes. If my previous essay relied more on Barth for the development of the *analogia fidei* for dialogue with the world, this discussion relies more on Bonhoeffer for a Christological cosmology and an ethic of concreteness; but, in any case, these two discussions must be regarded as a dual treatment of a single theme. My understanding of the therapeutic process remains, as in the earlier volume, more indebted to Rogers, existential psychology, and the American post-Freudian tradition than to earlier Freudian, Jungian, or behaviorist models. In general, this book is distinguished from *Kerygma and Counseling*, however, in two ways: it attempts (*a*) to deal critically with alternative prevailing options in the dialogue, and (*b*) to elaborate the implications of my thesis on the ontological assumptions of effective psychotherapy amid a rapidly secularizing historical situation.

My overall intention in this project on therapy may be expressed in another way in terms of an interpretation of the special problem and promise of American theology. The deep tragedy of the present madness of American theology (with its dead God, urban messianism, and exegetical atrophy) is that we have tried desperately to build a post-Barthian theology on a weak and eclectic foundation. American theology has bought Tillich without Barth, Reinhold Niebuhr without Barth, in the '50s we bought Bultmann without Barth, and now are in the process of buying Bonhoeffer without Barth. Each of these great theologians, however, made his contribution on the basis of a presupposed Barthian substructure, which has never been taken very seriously in America. Sadly enough, it is still less the exception than the rule for the American theological student to go through seminary, read three years in theology, and receive his B.D. without having ever read thoroughly a single volume of the preeminent theological work of our century, the *Church Dogmatics*. However far Continental theology may have departed from Barth in new hermeneutical, exegetical, and systematic directions, it has, nonetheless, remained in continuous creative dialogue with its foundation in the theology of the Word of God.[39] While I do not propose that American theology must slavishly follow the European pattern, I do protest its propensity to import selectively novel, current, and curious aspects of Continental theology, without a serious engagement with the deeper ground that it acknowledges, even when it exists in protest against that ground. If so, it may be that the most pressing theological homework for the American church is a belated encounter with the exegetical, historical, and systematic reflections of the mature Barth, admittedly laborious and repetitious, but always rewarding.

This general historical interpretation lies behind my decision to deal first with Barth, in the earlier volume, and only now with Bonhoeffer and his implications for the dialogue with therapy. Thus, if my effort is deliberately termed a post-Barthian engagement with psychotherapy, it in no sense seeks to be a rejection of the unfulfilled intentions of Barth's theological project, which centers in a Christological exegesis of reality, a project to which Bonhoeffer has contributed dramatically.

Frankly, I can only feel sadness at the way in which Bonhoeffer has been cheaply imported into the American religious market. With strong propensities toward anti-institutionalism, culture Protestantism, social messianism, and pragmatism, American readers have often managed to read Bonhoeffer with great selectivity. They buy his eth-

ics without his ecclesiology; they are ripe for his radical-
ism but are unimpressed by his talk of an arcane discipline;
they hear his call to worldly involvement but are deaf to
his Christological interpretation of the world. His questions about the possibility of a religionless Christianity
(essentially motivated by Barth's interpretation of Paul)
have been Americanized into a diatribe against the church.
His thoughts on a world come of age which lives without
using God as a *deus ex machina* have been reshaped into
a new American atheism that differs little from the Chau-
tauqua heydays of R. G. Ingersoll. His persistent concern
for vital exegesis has been buried under our journalisti-
cally oriented talk of the death of God. We have learned
to read selected portions of the prison letters without *Sanctorum Communio,* congenial bits of the *Ethics* without
The Cost of Discipleship, and the thesis on secularity without the exegetical struggle that produced it. We have good
reason to fear that the promise of church renewal in America, once so bright and real, may have been deceived by
this falsification and cheapening of Bonhoeffer into an esoteric messianism. Doubtless, some of our most brilliant
theological writers have been responsible for transmuting
Bonhoeffer into an American counterfeit. Similar dynamics, of course, have been at work in the Americanization of
Bultmann's theology.

If my thesis should prove correct, and if American theology is being called to take a " step backward " behind a
too-hasty and superficial dependence upon a de-Barthian-
ized Bonhoeffer, a dekerygmatized Bultmann, and a de-
ecclesiologized Tillich — a step backward to their own
rootage in a theology of the Word of God, and this means,
finally, a serious conversation with Barth — then my effort
at a theological interpretation of therapy can only serve as
a most elementary and tentative exploration of this path.
The task needs to be taken up on many fronts: exegetical,
historical, systematic, and practical. A careful study of
Bonhoeffer can help us to take these first steps.

CHAPTER III

The Divine Milieu

Père Teilhard de Chardin, French Jesuit paleontologist, philosopher of history, poet, mystic, and theologian, was, like Augustine and Luther, very much a man within and for the world, deeply engaged in dialogue with the structures of secular society, concerned not only with interpreting but with reshaping history. Teilhard's life embodied a bold and exciting style of "worldly theology" which frames certain profound questions for the emerging dialogue with psychotherapy. By worldly theology I mean a mode of reflection on the world that views the world exclusively as created, judged, and redeemed by God in Christ; that engages in a celebrative, Eucharistic relation with secularity on the assumption that Christ is the center of history; and that has learned to view the whole created order strictly and consistently under the image of redemption. It is worth noting that nearly a generation before Bonhoeffer (by 1927, although it remained unpublished until 1957), Teilhard had set forth a rather well developed conception of "the world come of age,"[1] had overcome the ever-present temptation of a high Christology to "think in terms of two spheres," yet without the dilution of theology to pantheism, and had set out on a heroic, autobiographically amazing life quest[2] to work out the implications of his crucial theological insight that matter embodies the word of God.

Père Teilhard, whose subtle influence has deeply shaped the course of Catholic renewal[3] and whose profound grasp of reality has magnetically captured the imagination of many scientifically oriented humanists,[4] was far ahead of his time in viewing the task of the church as that of pointing to the already-present action of God amid the secularizing process: " Christianity is not, as it is sometimes presented and sometimes practised, an additional burden of observances and obligations to weigh down and increase the already heavy load, or to multiply the already paralising ties of our life in society. It is, in fact, a soul of immense power which bestows significance and beauty and a new lightness on what we are already doing." [5] In a different language from Bonhoeffer's, but with similar intent, he argued for a kind of *naturaliter christiana*, Christocentrically interpreted, incognito within secularizing history.[6] For the new Catholic mind that celebrates modernity as existing within the divine milieu, there is " little to separate life in the cloister from life in the world." [7] " By means of all created things, without exception, the divine assails us, penetrates us and moulds us. We imagined it as distant and inaccessible, whereas in fact we live steeped in its burning layers. *In eo vivimus.*" [8] Our discussion can only serve as a brief glimpse into Teilhard's relevance for the dialogue with psychotherapy, and it is keenly hoped that it would be supplemented, as an appetizer is followed by a feast, by a careful perusal of Teilhard's own remarkable literary and scientific achievement.

1. CHRIST'S WORLDLY FORMATION

There is a profound delicacy in the intimate relation of the psychotherapeutic interview to which Teilhard speaks with great sensitivity: " Like those formidable physical forces which man has so disciplined that they can be made to carry out operations of amazing delicacy, so the enormous might of God's magnetism is brought to bear on our frail desires, our tiny objectives, without ever breaking their point." [9] So it is, if one views the therapeutic process from the vantage point of an understanding of Christ's taking form in the concrete history of the client in response to the empathetic love of God as mediated through the human brother, that the whole process may be viewed as a delicate operation of grace and freedom.

Such a perspective " introduces into our spiritual life a higher principle of unity, the specific effect of which can be seen — according to one's point of view — as either to make human endeavor holy or to make the Christian life fully human." [10] It is not therefore surprising that in *The Future of Man,* Teilhard identifies his theology as a " Christian humanism — faithful in this to the most firmly established theology of the Incarnation in which there is no real independence or discordance but a logical subordination between the genesis of humanity in the world and the genesis of Christ, through his Church, in humanity. Inevitably the two processes are structurally linked together, the second needing the first as the material on which it rests in order to supervitalize it." [11]

To a psychotherapist nurtured in such worldly theology, therefore, the created order manifests itself " as bathed in an inward light which brings out its structure, its relief, its depths. . . . The more completely the beings thus illumined attain to their natural fulfillment, the closer and more perceptible this radiance will be; and on the other hand, the more perceptible it becomes, the more clearly the contours of the objects which it bathes will stand out and the deeper will be their roots." [12] Such a therapist sees his client as if illuminated from within, the light as it were revealing the mystery of the process at work. The more fully his client attains his natural self-fulfillment, the more transparent the pattern of grace becomes, and the more clearly the pattern of grace is seen, the more adequately the person is known. Teilhard's consistent emphasis is upon the *visibility* of Christ's formation in the world, however, so that secular events are perceived without pantheistic reductionism as the face of God, the " aureole . . . through which is disclosed to us at every point of contact the unique essence of the universe." [13]

One might suppose with all his stress on Christ in the

world of *matter* that there would be in Teilhard the scientist a corresponding de-emphasis on the personal. To the contrary, it is precisely amid this cosmic movement of matter toward a " planetary consciousness " that we become aware, without loss of individual identity, that we are becoming " a single Somebody. For there is no total love — and this is writ large in the gospel — save that which is in and of the personal." [14]

But having already set forth Bonhoeffer's ethic of *forma Christi*, why now Teilhard's? Teilhard's unique contribution lies in his rich sensitivity to Christ's formation both in microcosm and macrocosm, in its intimacy and vastness, not only in personal history but in natural history, which he expresses with equal perceptiveness and assimilates within the framework of Catholic sacramental life and a dynamic transubstantiationalist tradition once so uniformly scorned by Protestants.

While Teilhard's contribution has already been widely recognized by natural scientists, biologists, paleontologists, and philosophers of history, we wish to pursue the promise of his work for the interpersonal sciences, chiefly those concerned with human growth toward authenticity, and especially psychotherapy. Teilhard was not a therapist, nor was he professionally concerned with healing relationships, yet in him we encounter a truly worldly and pastoral mentality that illuminates a theological and sacramental understanding of secular healing. But his special contribution to our theme is not through any clinical procedures or diagnostic insights for psychotherapy, but rather the comprehensive dimension of his theological vision of the world, a Christological cosmology which forms the contextual basis for a fuller anthropological reflection on sickness and health.

2. " THE MASS ON THE WORLD "

Of all Teilhard's enormously creative literary corpus, the piece we would select as the most forceful illustration of our theme is his deeply moving meditation " The Mass on the World," written in the Gobi Desert during his Chinese expedition of 1923. On the Feast of the Transfiguration, the faithful young priest found himself with neither bread nor wine for the celebration of the Mass. So deeply was he moved to fulfill his priestly service that he imaginatively submits to God a substitute offering of the whole material world which had been so deeply absorbing his thoughts as paleontologist and natural historian. Lacking ordinary Eucharistic elements, he turns his thoughts to the Eucharistic presence of Christ in the universe. The result is a shocking meditation in worldly piety. The meaning of transubstantiation, far from being minimized, is radicalized to the horizons of matter: " When Christ comes to one of his faithful it is not simply in order to commune with him as an individual: . . . when, through the mouth of the priest he says *Hoc est corpus meum,* . . . the effect of the priestly extends beyond the consecrated host to the cosmos itself." The sacramental presence of Christ is " aureoled with a real though attenuated divinizing of the entire universe." [15]

In what sense might such a sacramental cosmology impinge upon the therapeutic process? Effective therapeutic interaction already is uniquely suggestive of a " mass on the altar of the world " — suffering is being rehearsed, death and resurrection are embodied in speech, blood is being symbolically shed, a Communion is being enacted, bodies are broken and healed, and above all, psychotherapy is an act of remembrance.

Note carefully the simple shape of the priestly petition in the worldly Mass: " Since . . . I have neither bread, nor wine, nor altar, I will raise myself beyond these symbols, up to the pure majesty of the real itself; I, your priest, will make the whole earth my altar and on it will offer you all the labours and sufferings of the world. . . . I call before me the whole vast anonymous army of living humanity . . . this ocean of humanity whose slow monotonous wave-flows trouble the hearts even of those whose faith is most firm: it is to this deep that I thus desire all the fibres

of my being should respond . . . all of them, Lord, I try
to gather into my arms, so as to hold them out to you in
offering. This is the material of my sacrifice; the only material you desire." [16] The point is: The church offers to God
in the Mass the broken world. It is precisely this broken
world amid its struggle to understand itself which is the
subject of psychotherapy. Thus the church renders a service to secular healing that it may not choose to render
for itself: prayer. Nothing is left unpresented.

The scope of the sacramental act: " Over every living
thing which is to spring up, to grow, to flower, to ripen
during this day say again the words: This is my Body. And
over every death-force which waits in readiness to cor-
rode, to wither, to cut down, speak again your command-
ing words which express the supreme mystery of faith:
This is my Blood." [17] The offering presented: " The offering you really want, the offering you mysteriously need every day to appease your hunger, to slake your thrist, —
nothing less than the growth of the world borne ever on-
wards in the stream of universal becoming. Receive, O
Lord, this all-embracing host which your whole creation,
moved by your magnetism, offers you at this dawn of a
new day." [18] The vocational commitment presupposed in
all of this: " For me, my God, all joy and all achievement,
the very purpose of my being and all my love of life, all
depend on this one basic vision of the union between your-
self and the universe. Let others, fufilling a function more
august than mine, proclaim your splendours as pure Spirit;
as for me, dominated as I am by a vocation which springs
from the inmost fibres of my being, I have no desire, I
have no ability, to proclaim anything except the innumer-
able prolongations of your incarnate Being in the world of
matter; I can preach only the mystery of your flesh, you
the Soul shining forth through all that surrounds us." [19]

In Teilhard we encounter a sense of " unalloyed delight," an unquenchable thirst for discovery of the reality
that God is embodying to us in the here and now.[20] This is
a delight and thirst that well might constitute the deepest

motivation for both helper and sufferer in the therapeutic process as well.

Similarly the central theme of *Le Milieu Divin,* the "divinization of human activities and passivities," involves two motifs: (*a*) "the sanctification of human endeavour," and (*b*) "the humanization of christian endeavour." [21] The first views human processes (such as, for example, psychotherapy) in the context of the divine milieu, and the second views Christian commitment as humanized only through serious participation in the world. It is only through the mirror of the incarnation, however, that one can behold the colorful spectrum of worldly reality, and such processes as human healing as the embodiment of Christ's Lordship. "As a consequence of the Incarnation, the divine immensity has transformed itself for us into *the omnipresence of christification.*" He sharpens this remarkable point by saying: "Quite specifically it is Christ whom we make or whom we undergo in all things." [22]

If so, no psychotherapist does his work to himself. He exists in the divine milieu. "God reveals himself everywhere, beneath our groping efforts, as a *universal milieu. . . .* Each element of the world, whatever it may be, only subsists, *hic et nunc,* in the manner of a cone whose generatrices meet in God who draws them together." [23] It is precisely amid our worldly activities and passivities, and not in a flight from them, that the Word of God is embodied in and for the world. "By virtue of the Creation and, still more, of the Incarnation, *nothing* here below is profane for those who know how to see." [24]

The assertion that the world is in God, however, does not imply that God is synonymous with the world in a reductionist sense. In his imaginative modernization of the mystical tradition, Teilhard vigorously protests a pantheism that would reduce the whole life of God to "the face of God" (the world of matter). Much more interesting for our discussion, however, is the unique ground upon which he inveighs against pantheism: not so much on the basis that it denies God's reality, but that it denies the reality of the world! [25]

In an era in which some theologians have spoken in hushed tones of "the death of God," Teilhard gives us good reason to speak anew of the very process of elementary natural development as *forma Christi*. Over against antitheistic theologians who are convinced that God must be denied in order to affirm the world, Teilhard writes: "Without making the smallest concession to 'nature' . . . we can reconcile, and provide mutual nourishment for the love of God and the healthy love of the world." [26] Such an affirmation is rooted not only in the faith of the church but in wide empirical observation of the history of man and the study of archaeology, paleontology, astronomy, anthropology, and natural history.

3. TEILHARD AND BONHOEFFER

The differences between Teilhard and Bonhoeffer are surely obvious: Teilhard the sacramental scientist, Bonhoeffer the Lutheran exegete; Teilhard the natural historian, Bonhoeffer the theological ethicist; Teilhard the strangely mystical empiricist painstakingly working with detailed evidence, Bonhoeffer the political revolutionary sharing dramatically in the bloody upheavals of his day. But how similar they are in their interpretation of history, their affirmation of the world come of age, and the worldliness of the action of God! What a deep kinship can be seen in their cosmology, soteriology, and ethics. Both find crucial rootage in Col. 1:17.[27] Both are determined to be unassailably modern men, and yet at the same time traditioners of the apostolic witness within the context of modernity. How harmoniously does Teilhard (who wrote earlier and published later) symphonize the fragmented Bonhoefferian motifs of concreteness, reality, formation, nonreligious interpretation of Biblical concepts, the arcane discipline, radical discipleship, deputyship, and above all, a Christological cosmology! In the light of all this it is even more ironic that these two remarkable theologians

suffered similarly the cruelest rejection by and alienation
from the very historical and churchly structures they most
deeply loved.

Some may find it rather curious that we have chosen as
key theologians for focusing our dialogue with therapy
two who paid almost no attention whatsoever to psychotherapy in a structured sense, and if they had anything at
all to say about it, it tended to be witheringly negative or
derisively cutting. Yet it is ironic that these two men,
whose dramatic biographies attest to their ideas as something more than esoteric theorizing, perhaps hold greater
promise for the future dialogue with secular healing than
others less worldly and in a deeper sense less churchly.

The direction of our inquiry is now set. We are pursuing
a theological perception of the effective psychotherapeutic process as the incognito embodiment of Christ's formation in the secularizing world, using Barth's *analogia fidei*
to read the relation between God's self-disclosure in history and human self-disclosure in psychotherapy, Bonhoeffer's theology of the saeculum as a basis for viewing therapeutic formation, and Teilhard's sacramental cosmology as
an overarching framework for reflecting upon God's action in the evoluting world. My own position, which has
already been initially set forth in *Kerygma and Counseling*, is heavily indebted to these three theological initiatives. This constructive position will only emerge in sharp
focus, however, in relation to the prevailing patterns cur-
rently available, which I now intend critically to review.

PART TWO

PREVAILING PATTERNS:
A CRITIQUE

Among the numerous attempts of the last two decades to relate theology and therapy, three figures stand out above all others: Paul Tillich, Eduard Thurneysen, and Seward Hiltner. The three streams that follow after their efforts may without exaggeration be called the prevailing patterns in the dialogue today. Although reference to other writers varying in their significance may be found in our notes, this project would be quite incomplete without relating its concerns to the work of these three distinguished theologians. They not only typify the chief recurring motifs in the current dialogue, but in a broader sense most other available alternatives may be understood in terms of one of these three, or a combination of them.

The three types may be initially characterized in this way: (1) Tillich's method of correlation, i.e., correlating the existential questions of culture with the answers of theology, sets forth a pattern visibly reflected in numerous other theological interpreters of therapy who search for theological meanings embedded in the therapeutic process. (2) Thurneysen is the most respected and erudite representative of a significant group of kerymatic theologians writing on pastoral care (chiefly of the Lutheran and Reformed traditions) who have revitalized the older image of *Seelsorge* in the modern world, but who draw such sharp boundaries between pastoral conversation and psychotherapy that the implicit theological assumption of therapy is ignored, pastoral care is reduced to witnessing to the Word, and the dialogue is distorted by a strong polemical tendency. (3) Hiltner is the leading figure of American pastoral counseling, and remains the best exemplar of what he has called " operation-centered " pastoral theology, an orientation that would seek to derive theological insights from the examination of actual pastoral conversations and clinical relationships. The central *Problematik* of the larger group of pastors and chaplains surrounding Hiltner has been the search for a *modus vivendi* for concrete practical cooperation between religious and medical disciplines (especially psychiatry) with a view toward treatment of the whole man, a perspective widely held by most of the contributors to American pastoral care journals and the leadership of the clinical pastoral training movement.

It is especially unfortunate, if these are indeed the prevailing options, that none of them has embodied the core thrust of what we are calling worldly theology, with its high Christology and worldly conception of the Word of God, characterized by a determined refusal to see the world apart from Jesus Christ or Jesus Christ apart from the world. In each case the promise of an exegetically sound, confessionally congruent, guilelessly open dialogue with therapy has been aborted, either by thinking in terms of two spheres (Thurneysen), or by diluting the eventful character of the accepting reality (Tillich), or by reducing Christology to a purely functional matter (Hiltner).

We continue to witness a regrettable estrangement of American clinically oriented pastoral care from the exegetically oriented Continental tradition of pastoral care. The rich Lutheran tradition of pastoral care, which has matured amid Continental theology with a deeper soteriology than its American counterpart, has nonetheless been committed by the Lutheran doctrine of the two realms to a somewhat defensive attitude of striving to preserve the uniqueness of Christian pastoral care over against secular psychotherapy. It might profitably have learned from the

American experimental approach a greater sense of freedom for and openness to secular processes. While American pastoral care, on the other hand, has tended to develop good working relationships with medical resources through intensive clinical pastoral training in hospitals under staff supervision, it has been painfully crippled by a lack of deep theological self-awareness which might have matured in deeper ecumenical conversation. Furthermore, we have little reason to expect strong new initiatives to come from the school of Paul Tillich, with its increasing estrangement from the concrete life of the church, to reshape the dialogue between pastoral care and psychotherapy. If these three strands have developed somewhat independently, they doubtless need to complement one another at their weaker points.

It might appear, were we to pursue this line of thought, that the remainder of our discussion should become an attempt at a synthesis of these prevailing options. But that is far from the intention of this essay. They indeed need to complement one another, but even taken together with the best of each, they yet leave much to be desired. An additional new initiative is needed, and has already in part been supplied, unnoticed, by Bonhoeffer and Teilhard. The ensuing discussion attempts to spell out a critical appreciation of these prevailing stances, elaborated in the direction of a worldly theology. In order to sharpen this introductory statement, we shall begin with some categories which diagrammatically summarize these three positions and the correctives proposed in the light of new theological initiatives:

Prevailing Patterns:	THEOLOGY OF CULTURE (Tillich)	KERYGMATIC SEELSORGE (Thurneysen)	OPERATION-CENTERED PASTORAL THEOLOGY (Hiltner)
Contributions:	Ontology of Anxiety	Pastoral Care as Confession	Pragmatic Implementation of Therapeutic Attitudes

Limitations:	Ontological Reductionism	Kerygmatic Reductionism	Pragmatic Reductionism
	Dehistoricized Christology	Unworldly Christology	Functional Christology
	"Religion" as Theological Construct	Two-Sphere Thinking	Cultural Absorption
Corrective:	Nonreligious Interpretation of Biblical Concepts	Lordship of Christ in Secular Processes	Concrete Formation

It is much too simple a truism to suggest that these three viewpoints need one another as mutual correctives. What is more urgently needed is a perceptive integration of them on the basis of a Christology which is not really found in any of them, viz., a *worldly* (Bonhoefferian-Teilhardian) Christology, the outlines of which we have already set forth. Stated summarily: The central inadequacy of a theology of culture has been a *dehistoricized* Christology which misplaces the historicity of the accepting reality, the eventfulness of the power of acceptance. The central vacuity of the kerygmatic tradition has been its bent toward an *unworldly* or even antiworldly Christology that fails to celebrate the Lordship of Christ in the midst of universal history. The key weakness of operation-centered pastoral care is its *functional* Christology which has seemed content with accepting uncritically an already limited psychological interpretation of man (which may in turn make an occasional pragmatic "use" of theology, when expedient), coupled with a latitudinarian theological method which is used in that fashion without acting as watchful guardian of the authenticity of the Christian witness.

Put differently: If in Tillich we find a symbolic reduction of revelation in which contemporary culture inordinately preshapes the questions for revelation to answer in such a way that the hermeneutical circle is predominated by the current existential question (for that is the meaning of the principle of correlation), the process is exactly turned around in Thurneysen, so that the uniqueness of revelation in Jesus Christ is so narrowly defended as to neglect the presence of Christ amid the world, the result of which is a regrettable "thinking in terms of two spheres." If revelation at least remains a live issue for Tillich and Thurneysen, it hardly seems to be a vital problem in the American pragmatic tradition of pastoral care, which in the footsteps of Ritschl, Troeltsch, and Harnack has thought it could proceed quite as well without the excess baggage of Nicaea, Chalcedon, etc. It has been content to derive its "theological" bearings essentially from psychological case studies and clinical and pastoral relationships, the result of which is a *derivative* or functional theology, in which theology *functions* now and then to help out in the solution of some practical problem.

Thus we would hardly be well advised to call for a synthesis of these three traditions unless we specify which aspects we want to buy, otherwise we might merely produce a synthesis of the antisecular tendency of the kerygmatic tradition, the anti-exegetical bent of the pragmatic tradition, and the antihistorical bent of Tillich's ontology. We need Hiltner's pragmatic openness but with deeper Christological identity, Thurneysen's exegetical integrity but with a direction facing toward the world, and Tillich's existential probing but undergirded by a demythologized Chalcedonian Christology. The posthumously published Bonhoeffer (*Ethics* and *Letters*) supplements Tillich's religious ontology with a much more fascinating proposal for a "religionless" Christianity and a worldly affirmation of the kerygma, corrects Thurneysen's introversion with a Christological affirmation of the secular and Hiltner's functionalism with a Christological interpretation of concreteness (that Christ takes shape in concrete interpersonal relationships). To support these criticisms and to clarify our alternative is now our task.

CHAPTER IV

Tillich's Theology of Culture

The kinship between psychotherapy, existentialism, and theology is a recurrent theme in Paul Tillich's thought, appearing repeatedly in *The Courage to Be, Theology of Culture, Systematic Theology,* and numerous essays.[1] His thoughts on this subject have been read more seriously by the religiously disinterested and quoted by a broader spectrum of Protestant and Catholic writers than have those of any other contemporary theologian. His passing is a grievous loss to the continuing theological conversation with the healing arts. In some ways, Tillich's work comes close to fulfilling Bonhoeffer's call for an openness to secular culture, an abolition of the rigid boundary between sacred and secular, and a theological interpretation of history in a world come of age. Yet, so very different is it from the exegetical, ethical, and ecclesiological thrust of the Bonhoefferian direction we have set for ourselves that careful attention must be given to clarifying these differences.

Tillich's lifelong concern has been with a theological analysis of culture and history. He has astutely shown how contemporary art, philosophy, psychotherapy, and history raise the human questions that an adequate theology must seek to answer.

Tillich has searched for new language and symbols in contemporary cultural forms that express the Christian understanding of man's estrangement and healing. According to Tillich, psychoanalysis provides us with just such a new framework and set of symbols for grasping the human pre-

dicament and the reality of the Christian life. We will proceed with a critical explication of his views.

1. THE HERMENEUTICS OF CORRELATION

Tillich's extraordinarily lucid essay on " Psychoanalysis,
Existentialism and Theology " concludes with this doxo-
logical mandate: " Theology has received tremendous gifts
from existentialism and psychoanalysis, gifts not dreamed
of fifty years ago or even thirty years ago. We have these
gifts. Existentialists and analysts themselves do not need
to know that they have given to theology these great
things. But the theologians should know it." [2] However
true it may be that Christian theology is called to celebrate
secular gifts, we have reason to believe that behind such
a statement lies a more serious theological resignation to
the fact that the church has no special *witness* in any
unique way to secularity in general or therapy in particular, but that it can rest quite content to receive the fruits
and succor of psychotherapy's table, digesting them into a
general anthropology without ever getting around to an
authentic two-way dialogue involving a specific witness to
the therapist concerning the source of the acceptance
which he daily employs, insofar as his therapy is effective.
Hence, we set forth our first proposition vis-à-vis Tillich:
*If the conversation with therapy is to transcend a one-way
monologue in which psychology frames the questions for
theology to answer, theology must not become captive to
a theological method whose hermeneutic already predis-
poses it against the questions framed by God's own self-
disclosure, but rather, in a definite sense the reality of God
must come to frame the deeper ontological and anthropological questions for psychotherapy.* To support our proposition, we must show how Tillich's thought on this subject
has, unintentionally, had a monological (*nondialogical*)
tendency (lacking *marturia*), and in what sense his theological method (the principle of correlation) is actually
responsible for this, before we can proceed toward a constructive statement.

The overwhelming importance of psychoanalysis for contemporary theology is seen in Tillich's essay on " The Theological Significance of Existentialism and Psychoanalysis ": " Theology had to learn from the psychoanalytic method the meaning of grace." But specifically, what does psychoanalysis have to learn from the Christian witness? Of this we hear nothing. Consistently, the stream of learning flows in one direction: " The word grace, which had lost any meaning, has gained a new meaning by the way in which the analyst deals with his patient. He accepts him. He does not say, ' You are acceptable,' but he accepts him. And that is the way in which, according to religious symbolism, God deals with us." [3] However we might agree with the intent of such a statement, is it not more urgent in our situation to reverse the question and allow the analogy to move toward therapy instead of merely away from it? What can the therapist learn about the source and meaning of acceptance by looking toward its ontological ground in the event of divine self-disclosure to which Christian witness points? We wish to ask how far a thoroughly confessional theology admits of genuine hardheaded dialogue with the presuppositions of other scientific and medical viewpoints, which are, finally, just as confessional as the Christian witness. Perhaps the shape of the recent dialogue between Marxists and Christians in East Germany [4] provides us with the most vital and edifying pattern for the quality of candid dialogue for which we search with psychotherapy. Theology is called to engage in conversation with the healing arts on just such a frank confessional basis, not first of all looking for " common ground " within the framework of a limited anthropology while paying the price of forgetting from the outset its distinctive self-understanding, but willing to listen, and calling our partners in dialogue to listen to themselves at the level of depth at which God himself hears and understands.

Tillich's theological method is based upon the principle of correlation: correlating culture's questions with the answers of revelation. Theology's task is to listen to culture frame the human question and to bring to bear religious symbolism as it correlates with man's existential questions.[5] It is not surprising, therefore, that psychotherapy should become for Tillich a major resource for speaking of the human condition, and thus a wellspring for theological reflection, since it grapples daily with man's existential questions. Many of us have become accustomed to thinking of Tillich's method as uniquely helpful for dialogue with culture, but we wish to raise a serious query as to whether it might actually be more a foil, a slightly diverting circumvention of the deepest sort of dialogue.

Certainly a basic commitment of Tillich's method of correlation is that it is impossible to receive an answer to questions man has never asked.[6] This seems to imply, if taken quite seriously, that any meaningful revelation of God must be utterly dependent upon our first asking the questions (of our finitude, guilt, etc.) that may lead us toward revelation. We prefer, instead, to proceed in an entirely different direction which assumes that God speaks whether or not we hear him, acts whether or not we consciously share in his action, bestows himself to us regardless of whether we choose ourselves as recipients of his self-bestowal. Vis-à-vis therapy, God's unconditional positive regard is present as the ontological ground of our own positive regard, however much we may fail to perceive it. If this is so, then would not authentic dialogue with the therapist consist more in listening to the patient so as to point him unmistakably toward the ground upon which he already stands rather than place him on new ground through a more skillful " interpretation of religious symbolism "?[7] If it should be the case that the revelation of God puts its own questions to man so as to transform all his human questions, then would not authentic dialogue consist, at least in part, in clarifying the sense in which the self-disclosure of God itself reframes the very questions of the dialogue, instead of proceeding exclusively on the basis of sinful man's myopic self-questioning?

If so, we must candidly recognize from the outset that Tillich's theological method does not begin with what, in our view, is the legitimate and proper wellspring of the best Christian thinking about man, culture and reality, sickness and health, viz., the divine self-disclosure. Tillich, instead, has insisted that there is another and better place to start — the existential condition of man, " prior to revelation," if that is conceivable.

2. " Logos Asarkos "

This brings us to our next crucial issue with Tillich, which finds its focus in the following thesis for discussion: *Dialogue with therapy on its implicit Christological center cannot mature fully on the basis of an exegetically questionable adoptionist Christology, since any theology which dilutes the full, eventful participation of the incarnate God in the world finally ends with a denial of the reality of the world and not merely an innocuous Christological dilution.* However instructive and thought-provoking Tillich's systematic theology has been for us, the overall weakness of the system lies precisely at the heart of it in an anemic Christological affirmation that never quite comes to grips either with the New Testament Messianic confessions or with classical patristic Christological thought. Tillich's Christ is a *logos asarkos*, a fleshless Christ, a nonhistorical idea. Our dissatisfaction with Tillich can be put clearly by simply saying that any attempt to speak of Christian revelation without the *name* " Jesus Christ " fails by falling into an *asarkos* Christology. The name Jesus Christ points to a person and an event that cannot properly be dehistoricized.[8] The Word of God of which the New Testament speaks is always a Word made flesh, and therefore a worldly Word. To speak of the courage to accept one's acceptance is fine, but Tillich's inclination to propose a redeemed self-understanding while leaving behind the historical event that calls forth this self-understanding should be avoided.

Since the doctrinal focus of our whole discussion of

therapeutic empathy has been the incarnation, it is necessary to comment specifically on Tillich's critique of such
incarnational thinking. It was Tillich who wrote: " The assertion that ' God has become man ' is not a paradoxical
but a nonsensical statement. It is a combination of words
which makes sense only if it is not meant to mean what
the words say. . . . The only thing God cannot do is to
cease to be God." [9] Tillich cautiously affirms the Johannine
statement that the *logos* became flesh only on the condition that *logos* be vaguely defined as " the principle of the
divine self-manifestation in God as well as in the universe,
in nature as well as in history." [10] But even such bland language must be used sparingly, since it is " practically impossible to protect the concept from superstitious conno-
tations." [11]

What Tillich substitutes for traditional ecumenical
(Chalcedonian) Christology often appears to be little more
than a psychologizing of Jesus facing anxiety on the basis
of an amorphous adoptionism. Although he has rightly argued for the genuine participation of Jesus in the depths
of human estrangement (in loneliness, temptation, finitude, anxiety over death, etc.), he successfully evades
commitment at the one point that seemed so obvious to
the remembering church of the New Testament, viz., that
" God was in Christ " (II Cor. 5:19), that " in him all the
fullness of God was pleased to dwell " (Col. 1:19), that
here we encounter God himself participating in our human condition. The significance of Jesus' ministry was not
merely that human initiative was conquering estrangement under the conditions of existence (although indeed
it was that), but the fact that God himself was taking radical initiative to engage himself fully in our estranged human situation, even unto death. This is the heart of the
Christology which enables us to develop a serious analogy
with therapeutic empathy (as radical participation in the
situation of another), but regrettably it is unthinkable on
the basis of Tillich's Christology.

If a weak link exists at the crucial point of Christology

in a theological system, it is sure to weaken the entire remainder of the chain of argument. Just such a weak link exists in Tillich's system in his repeated assertion that the act of God hinges upon the reception of man, in effect making the love of God dependent upon human knowledge, volition, and courage. For "without this reception the Christ would not have been the Christ." [12] Unmistakably, Tillich argues the dependence of Christ upon the church in this inverted formula: "The Christ is not the Christ without those who receive him as the Christ." [13]

This dialectic, which is not an incidental statement but plays a central role in Tillich's Christology, runs counter to the New Testament celebration of the God who is for us in Christ, whether we accept him or not, and indeed in spite of all human rejection (Eph. 2:4-18; Rom. 8:35-39), a view which can already be found formally in the Old Testament as well (Hos. 1:2 ff.). It is strictly upon this basis that we have argued analogically that therapeutic acceptance has its ground in the acceptance of God, which does not depend upon our reception of it for its efficacy.

Tillich's most exaggerated reductionist formula, however, is found in his well-known statement that "Christology is a function of soteriology." [14] If Christology is defined as the systematic study of the meaning of the Christ and soteriology as the inquiry into the meaning of salvation and of our reception of the deed of God in the Christ, we can only conclude from this that Jesus Christ is important theologically or personally merely to the degree to which he functions to bring us to a new way of being. The logic of the New Testament is exactly opposite, however: The only reason the Gospels and Epistles are concerned at all with our possibility for a new way of being (soteriology) is that we have been met in a renewing event by one (the subject of Christology) who enables us to speak of a "new being."

3. ONTOLOGICAL REDUCTIONISM

Since our discussion of the implicit ontological assumption of effective psychotherapy is deeply akin to and in part indebted to Tillich's thought on "the power of acceptance," we must now clarify Tillich's view and our response to it. The most crucial passage that anticipates our proposal appears in *The Courage to Be:*

In the communion of healing, for example the psychoanalytic situation, the patient participates in the healing power of the helper by whom he is accepted although he feels himself unacceptable. The healer, in this relationship, does not stand for himself as an individual but represents the objective power of acceptance and self-affirmation.[15]

This passage sets the stage for our third proposition, which argues that *any theology of acceptance which proposes a congruent dialogue with therapeutic acceptance must be completely explicit and unconcealed about its understanding of the source of the accepting reality, its eventful character in Jesus Christ, and must not allow the event of divine acceptance to become vaguely dehistoricized into the general idea of acceptance, or the act of faith reduced to a genre of existentialist courage.*

What does Tillich mean by " the objective power of acceptance "? In the same passage, he argues that " the ultimate power of self-affirmation can only be the power of being-itself." [16] But we ask, exactly what does this signify, and how does this power of " being-itself " make itself known in history concretely and believably? Does the power of acceptance take any special initiative to clarify itself before men's eyes, to disclose itself once for all so that the "mystery hidden for ages and generations " is " now made manifest " (Col. 1:26)? These are questions for which the New Testament witness exists as an answer. But Tillich's responses are, for the most part, either semantically vacuous or clouded with ambiguities. We are convinced that the dialogue with therapy cannot afford to be ambiguous or diversionary precisely at this point, since here is where theology can make its most significant contribution by pointing explicitly to the event character of the self-disclosure of the accepting reality, which is implicitly presupposed in effective therapy.

In this connection, it is now possible for us to clarify what we mean by Tillich's *ontological reductionism*. It is his propensity to absorb revelation into a general doctrine of being, faith into an ontology of courage, and God into an impersonal view of " being-itself." The ontology, which at first appears to be promising for the dialogue with therapy, is found to have unexpectedly ruinous consequences. Tillich seems all too willing to speak of faith without the event (Jesus Christ) that calls it forth. In fact, " faith cannot even guarantee the name ' Jesus ' in respect to him who was the Christ. It must leave that to the incertitudes of our historical knowledge." [17]

Our suspicions about the dehistoricizing propensity of Tillich's concept of faith are fully confirmed when he writes: " The faith which creates the courage to take them [doubt and meaninglessness] into itself has no special content. It is simply faith, undirected, absolute. It is undefinable, since everything defined is dissolved by doubt and meaninglessness." [18] It may be surprising that a theologian who has spent so much of his career with an analysis of history should be called nonhistorical in a certain sense. I hope it is clear, however, that the particular sense in which I understand Tillich to be exhibiting a dehistoricizing bias is in the crucial question of Christology. I find him quite willing to speak of the idea of acceptance without speaking in the same breath of the event of acceptance. The process of coming "to accept this power of acceptance consciously " is dealt with under the category of *absolute faith,* but this, in the last analysis, also becomes " *a faith which has been deprived by doubt of any concrete content.*" [19] This is the special meaning we attach to the term " ontological reductionism."

4. EXISTENTIAL AND PATHOLOGICAL ANXIETY

Now we turn to a less subtle, more pragmatic issue: *The boundary between existential and pathological anxiety cannot be accepted as the proper distinction between pastoral and medical services, if both services are directed to the whole man.* This proposition is offered under the conviction that theology must combat the professionalizing tendency, so evident in current medical practice, by not allowing itself to become a partner to a theoretical or actual division of man.

Tillich has persuasively criticized both medical and theological faculties on the grounds that the medical faculties (especially psychiatry) have not developed an integral doctrine of man upon which to base their healing arts, while theological faculties have failed to develop an ontology of anxiety and acceptance. He calls for cooperation between the faculties of medicine and theology on the basis of certain highly debatable principles, one of which is as follows: " Pathological anxiety, once established, is an object of medical healing. Existential anxiety is an object of priestly help." [20] If pastoral care, however, is directed toward the human sickness, and if psychotherapy deals with overarching categories of human existence, then we have good reason to believe that both medical and ministerial functions will be validly concerned with pathological *and* existential anxiety.

The distinction might be drawn more circumspectly in this way: The therapist *mediates*, through his empathetic activity, the healing power of " being-itself," whereas Christian proclamation *announces* the concrete, trustable self-disclosure of that power of acceptance. It is entirely conceivable that a therapist might momentarily cease his distinctive therapeutic relationship and occasionally speak overtly to his client of the source of the healing reality upon which they both depend. He might even mount a pulpit from time to time and speak confessionally of the self-disclosure of the accepting reality. But it is not necessary for him to verbalize it in order to mediate it interpersonally. On the other hand, the minister, who is called more specifically to participate in the overt clarification, through word and Sacrament, of the event of God's occurring love, is likewise called to mediate that love congruently and empathetically in interpersonal relationships. But this, of course, is the vocation of every man. The parish minister may not be so skillful in mediating unconditional positive regard as the professional psychotherapist who, day after day, is involved in refining such a relationship; but he is, nonetheless, called to strive toward precisely the same attitude. Whether professional or unsophisticated, whether medical or pastoral, the helping person will mediate an unconditional positive regard that is rooted in reality itself, but the client has a right to expect from a trained and experienced professional a more skillful mediation of empathetic understanding, whereas the pastor may be in the long run freer to proclaim the *event* through which the reality of acceptance has made itself known to us in history.

Tillich's boundary between medicine and religion comes close to springing the trap against which Bonhoeffer warned, viz., of thinking in terms of two spheres, of trying to secure some ground for religious healing over against secular healing. In an argument designed to show that psychotherapy cannot heal the existential estrangement of man, e.g., he writes: " They try with their methods to overcome existential negativity, anxiety, estrangement, meaninglessness, or guilt. They deny that they are universal, that they are existential in this sense. They call all anxiety, all guilt, all emptiness, illnesses which can be overcome as any illness can be, and they try to remove them. But this is impossible. The existential structures cannot be healed by the most refined techniques. They are objects of salvation." [21] Yet it is undeniable that much recent psychotherapy — following Binswanger, von Gebsattel, von Weizsäcker, Frankl, van den Berg, Boss, and others [22] — is increasingly concerning itself, and not with

out success, with just such existential negativities as meaninglessness and emptiness; and, needless to say, guilt and
anxiety have long been objects of psychotherapeutic help.

Again in " The Theology of Pastoral Care," Tillich deals
with the jurisdictional issue between the functions of ministry and psychotherapy, but the boundary is carelessly
drawn: " As the minister should not try to make healing
his function, neither should the psychotherapist exercise
pastoral care as his function." [23] This seems to stand in direct contrast to what I take to be his more considered
judgment, best expressed in his sermon " On Healing," that
all healing has to do with the whole man and that the
skillful doctor will minister to the whole person: " The
great physician is he who does not easily cut off parts and
does not easily suppress the one function in favor of the
other, but he who strengthens the whole so that within
the unity of the body the struggling elements can be reconciled." [24] This point is stated even more sharply in Vol.
III of *Systematic Theology*, where he has written: " Health
and salvation are identical, both being the elevation of
man to the transcendent unity of the divine life. . . .
Health in the ultimate sense of the word, health as identical with salvation, is life in faith and love." [25] Our problem
with such a bald equation of salvation and health is not
that we disagree etymologically or that we wish to retreat
to " thinking in terms of two spheres," but that we do not
want uncritically to identify a limited definition of health
with a broader interpretation of salvation, or a narrow
view of salvation with a more profound view of health. If
salvation has essentially to do with our response to God's
action, and health has to do with human well-functioning,
surely these must be distinguished but not separated. For
we suspect that the relatively well functioning person,
who (perhaps through psychotherapy) has been enabled
to overcome neurotic anxieties and guilts and exists in
openness to himself and others, is (in a fragmented but
nevertheless recognizable way) manifesting the very style
of life which is hoped for and in some sense received and

understood in the Christian community as salvation.

The deeper clue, however, to the distinction for which
we are grappling is the difference (unnoted by Tillich but
fully developed by Barth, *CD*,IV/2) between *de jure* and
de facto health or *salvus*, viz., God has given humanity
health in Jesus Christ. All men already participate in this
healthy act. Eschatologically (before the end-time verdict
of God already proleptically present in Jesus Christ) and
de jure (by this divine verdict), all men are before God
made whole, healed, renewed; and yet we do not always
actualize in our behavior and decisions (*de facto*, as a matter of fact) that full-functioning health for which we are
intended and freed by the event of God's love.[26] Jesus
Christ has functioned in our place. He is our health (*salvus*). We are clothed in his health. God views us as healthy
in him. The beginning point of a Christian doctrine of
health is thus God's own therapeutic deed. But whether
we actualize this health in our own existence is a matter
for us daily to decide in response to the divine decision.

5. EXPANDING THE DIALOGICAL AGENDA

To this we must add a final thesis for discussion in relation to Tillich's contribution: *The theological engagement
with therapy must not be content with its present focus
upon comparative anthropologies, the diagnosis of the human predicament, and the pathology of the human boundary situation, but must instead redirect the discussion
toward an ontology of health, reconciliation, and redemption, and the more difficult yet promising issues of Christology and ecclesiology as legitimate for the dialogical
agenda.*

Bonhoeffer's basic quarrel with "boundary situation"
theology, such as that of Tillich, is the subtle assumption
that God seems to be working on the edge of life, just at
the abyss of human meaninglessness and doubt where man
is at the end of his rope, but not at the center of ordinary
existence, not in the middle of town. Bonhoeffer rightly
calls us to listen for the speech of God not merely in this

or that special *kairos* of history, but in the totality of history; not in the limitations and predicament of man only or " at the boundary," but at the center of human existence; not at man's point of weakness only, but also at his point of strength.

Significantly, Tillich once admitted that his only basic quarrel with his " great and wonderful friend, Karen Horney," centered on the question of whether man has an essential thrust toward health. Horney believed that even amid his neurotic compulsions man has a persistent impulse toward self-actualization, as do Maslow and Rogers today.[27] It is interesting that both Bonhoeffer and Teilhard share the same basic intuition of Horney (although setting it in the revolutionizing context of a Christological cosmology) over against the more pessimistic and Freudianly oriented theological tradition of Tillich and Reinhold Niebuhr. Elsewhere we have criticized Tillich's creation gnosticism, which argues that " actualized creation and estranged existence are identical," in tension with the Biblical doctrine that creation is good.[28] With this doctrine of creation, one is not surprised that in his dialogue with psychotherapy Tillich was always much more drawn to Freud with his interest in the irrational element, human estrangement, and " the geography of hell," than toward therapists such as Künkel and Rogers, who see human estrangement only in the light of authenticity and health.

Tillich has often spoken of the aim of psychotherapy as enabling man to " accept himself in all his negativities," [29] but we must ask whether the estranged needs to learn to accept himself also in his positive goodness and authentic intentionality. Not merely guilt and anxiety and meaninglessness, but also long-submerged feelings of love, trust, and openness must be brought into conscious awareness in psychotherapy. Tillich's limited definition of the therapeutic task as that of accepting the negativities of existence without removing them is closely related to his equally limited description of the Christ as one who " accepts the negativities of existence without removing them." [30]

So preoccupied is Tillich with the existentialist syndrome of negativity and estrangement that in one essay on "Theology and Counseling" he advises that a crucial implication of theology for counseling is that it will call the counselor to discuss with the troubled person the fact that he himself exists under the same predicament of guilt, anxiety, and limitation. "This may be done by telling a concrete story in which the counselor experienced the same negativities for which the counselee needs care."[31] This sort of introversion easily becomes unhelpful therapy, however, shifting the focus of therapeutic conversation away from the internal situation of the troubled individual and toward the wholly different frame of reference of the counselor with his often unanalogous conflicts and inconsistencies.

In sum, whereas Tillich has focused more specifically upon the ontological dimension of the human predicament and pathology, we share the hope of many today for a broadening of the agenda in the dialogue with psychotherapy, so as also to include a phenomenology of health, the ontological assumptions of therapeutic effectiveness, the healing process and its relation to the therapeutic act of God. We have reason to believe that the *analogia fidei* offers the most helpful theological tool for broadening this agenda.[32]

Chapter V

Thurneysen's Kerygmatic *Seelsorge*

The second prevailing pattern with which we find ourselves in unavoidable dialogue is that of the distinguished pastor, teacher, and associate of Barth, Eduard Thurneysen. His monumental volume on *A Theology of Pastoral Care* appears to be the outstanding work of the past generation in pastoral care based on the kerygmatic tradition. More forcefully than others who have written on this subject, Thurneysen has discussed the task of pastoral care in the light of God's pastoral care for us. Although a keen and knowledgeable student of Freudian analysis as well as of analytical psychology, he unfortunately has never turned his attention toward developments in American psychotherapy, especially toward Sullivan, Rogers, and Maslow and their theological significance. As with so many Continental scholars, the German academic tradition has proved to be so rich for him that he has failed to turn his attention to developments elsewhere.

1. TWO-SPHERE THINKING

Despite its many achievements, Thurneysen's theology of pastoral care is burdened by an unnecessary cynicism toward all secular healing. We are convinced that this cynicism can be averted, not by a Christological dilution, but by a deeper Christology that celebrates Christ's concrete formation in the world.

While Thurneysen broadly argues that the object of pastoral care is the totality of man's personal existence,[1] he narrowly speaks of the church as the exclusively appropriate context for the care of souls. Although we agree that "pastoral care occurs within the realm of the church," [2] we wish also to show that the church's true ministry is in and for the world, and that the world's own care for its own may already have implicit theological assumptions. Accordingly, our first proposition for discussion is: *The post-Bonhoefferian dialogue with psychotherapy must repudiate the tendency of much traditional* Seelsorge *to " think in terms of two spheres," bifurcating reality into sacred and secular healing so as to lose sight of the implicit theological presuppositions of psychotherapy, or to protect some privileged " space " in the rapidly secularizing world for introverted religiosity.*

Doggedly Thurneysen has argued that the shakiest foundation upon which pastoral care might build is " modern psychotherapy." There is no doubt about his intention to effect a strict separation between churchly and worldly healing. " No real pastoral care is possible from this ground; only some secular form of common sense." [3] In order to minister to the troubled man " we shall do everything to transfer his concerns from the human and psychological realm into the quite different realm disclosed by the Word of God." [4]

His two-sphere thinking reveals itself most sharply in the firm boundary he draws between sin and neurosis: " Each belongs to its own order: the neurosis to the immanent and natural, sin to the transcendent. Sin is something *toto genere* other than neurosis." [5] He argues that " modern psychotherapy is of an essentially secular nature," [6] that one should " beware of confounding a successful psychotherapeutic cure with repentance," and that psychotherapy and pastoral care are " *toto genere* and unexchangeably different." [7]

We will not repeat our reasons for viewing psychotherapy as implicitly akin to the kerygma, but we cannot fail to note that it is not merely pragmatic considerations but also Christological and exegetical considerations which persuade us that pastoral care can proceed in much the same fashion as effective client-centered therapy, always free to proclaim the gospel contextually, but also free to listen empathetically without the Word being overtly spoken. The basic issue at stake here is whether the love of God must be mediated verbally, or may be mediated through a concrete interpersonal relationship without the overt proclamation of the gospel. We find unconvincing Thurneysen's claims that the processes of psychotherapy and pastoral care are " *toto genere* and unexchangeably different."

Despite his polemic against pietism, Thurneysen tends against his own deepest intuition to become ensnared in a pietistic syndrome of defensiveness that seeks to preserve a special realm for a specifically religious therapy in a world come of age. The territory he would preserve is " sin and grace." Employing a thoroughly Kantian bifurcation between empirical and a priori knowledge, he writes: " The concepts of sin and grace have no place in a scientific, psychological description of life. If they are employed there, they are improperly, even illegally employed." [8] Yet this seems not to have anticipated the fact that there might develop a rather significant school of psychotherapy which argues that it is impossible to understand psychopathic, psychotic, and neurotic behavior *without* the construct of sin, a school that is already forcefully developing in America with Mowrer and his followers.[9]

Although Thurneysen criticizes the philosophical presuppositions of scientific empiricism, he confusingly confines the work of psychology to the restricted empiricism that he has just rejected, thus ignoring the difficult struggle in which many existential psychotherapists (von Gebsattel, Caruso, Boss, *et al.*) are engaged against precisely this narrow empiricism. A large group of American psychologists (led by Maslow, Moustakas, Rogers, and May) are also involved in the same struggle.[10] A theology committed to dialogue is surely called more to give aid and

comfort to their cause than to rail against their transgres-
sion of a strict empiricism.

Thurneysen speaks of the " self-sufficiency of true pastoral care," presumably cut off from dependence upon any
secular wisdom. Rather extremely, he argues that Christian pastoral care "must critically dissociate itself from
the essentially alien philosophical presuppositions inherent in psychology." [11] " In contrast to the psychoanalytic
conversation, the pastoral conversation proceeds in strict
and fundamental dependence on Holy Scripture." [12] It is
thus not surprising that Thurneysen should finally regard
psychotherapy as a potentially " dangerous poison " [13] that
can open up wounds which only pastoral care can heal.

Over against such a strict diastasis, we are convinced
that the church's ministry to the world may and must
freely and pragmatically utilize the insights, procedures,
and attitudes of effective psychotherapy, always maintaining a critical stance toward hidden philosophical presuppositions at work behind various theories of therapy, but
nevertheless free (as was the early church) to claim the
best human wisdom for the service of the church. More
so, however, theology is called to point to the implicit ontological presuppositions and ontic commitments of therapy that are already inconspicuously akin to the Christian
proclamation, and in this as every other realm, " take every
thought captive " to Christ.[14]

2. CONVERSATIONAL PREACHING

Closely related to this point is our second proposition:
*The reshaping of pastoral care must resist the temptation
to reduce pastoral help to merely another form of preaching, just as the theological dialogue with psychotherapy
must not try to reduce the essence of therapy to some form
of proclamation.* If therapy implicitly presupposes the accepting reality explicitly declared in preaching, then there
can be no doubt of the intimate, yet hidden relation between good pastoral therapy and the clear and effective
proclamation of the gospel. But an uncritical identifica-

tion of preaching and pastoral care is beneficial to neither. The formula for their proper relationship may be stated summarily: Pastoral care mediates interpersonally and often without verbal proclamation the accepting reality which preaching explicitly clarifies as having its ground and source in Jesus Christ.

Over against this view it is clear that Thurneysen, in the last analysis, flatly reduces pastoral care to a form of preaching. Pastoral conversation, he says, must deal exclusively with " the Word of God *pronounced* in a specific way among men." [15] It fails altogether if it speaks merely of " profane " things. It is only as " this dialogue between two men, started perhaps entirely on the profane level, succeeds in submitting the partners to the authority of the Word of God," that " a true pastoral conversation has been achieved." [16] If so, it is difficult to see how pastoral care is anything more than mere *conversational preaching*.

This kerygmatic reductionism reaches its climax where Thurneysen quotes with approval Asmussen's definition of pastoral care as the " ' proclamation of the Word of God from man to man ' in the form of a conversation in which ' the message is told to the individual face to face.' " [17] Thurneysen summarizes his own definition as follows: " Pastoral counseling happens in the form of a conversation — listening to the Word of God and responding to the Word of God." [18] We can agree, at an incognito level, that effective therapy secular or otherwise consists finally in listening for the Word of God speaking implicitly *through* the concrete interpersonal relationship, but this Word need not be made verbally explicit in order to be effectual and concrete.

Thurneysen employs no such distinction between implicit and explicit, and the whole tenor of his argument would lead one to believe he would resist it strongly. Anything short of overt kerygmatic proclamation is " merely sophisticated, philosophical or poetic talk." He rejects the whole process in which one " person bares his soul to another " as romantic.[19] " Pastoral care can be nothing else

than a communication of the Word of God in a particular
form. Hence, pastoral care can be concerned with nothing
else than the proclamation of forgiveness and the sanctification of man for God." [20] Our basic issue, however, is
whether the Word can be the Word without being articu-
lated by man — curiously enough the same issue we face
with Tillich's Christology, but in an entirely different
guise. Thurneysen's whole line of argument is sorely
tempted, despite itself, to take the Word of God captive,
limit it only to that occasion in which it is captured in
man's speech, as if the Word were not effectually present
amid the structures of the world and even amid the notori-
ous failures of human works and words.

3. THE LOSS OF EMPATHY

*A thoroughgoing critique of natural theology does not
necessitate a denial of empathy.* In *Kerygma and Counseling,* I applied Barth's *analogia fidei* to the dialogue with
therapy, affirming his penetrating critique of natural theology which rejects any standpoint that would begin its interpretation of man and God from some point other than
God's self-disclosure. Now I find myself in the anomalous
position of defending Barth's position over against that of
his old friend and fellow revolutionary, Thurneysen, who
clearly interprets the critique of natural theology as a rejection of empathy.

Empathy, which involves the process of participating in
the frame of reference of the estranged neighbor, is best
understood theologically under the analogy of God's incarnate love which assumes the frame of reference of finite
and estranged humanity, even unto death.[21] Thurneysen,
however, argues that " if we join the counselee — perhaps
only tentatively and experimentally — on the ground from
which he first comes, we base our pastoral care not on the
Word but on a secular understanding of man and on a corresponding ' natural theology.' " [22] Whereas empathy intends to take with full seriousness the inner distortions of
the troubled neighbor, Thurneysen advises oppositely that

we direct him *away* from his own feelings and *toward* "the quite different realm disclosed by the Word of God." Only this determines "the worth or worthlessness of our pastoral care." [23] For "God's Word does not lie somewhere in the depths of the human soul, waiting to be awakened, perhaps with the help of the Bible." [24] Thurneysen is only partially right to quote, in support of this view, Barth, who insists that the Word of God lies at the depths of all creation whose center is the covenant which is clarified once for all in Jesus Christ, and that we are called to take the troubled and imprisoned neighbor as seriously as God has taken him.[25] Therefore, we can hardly agree with Thurneysen that God's Word is *always* strictly a *verbum alienum*, utterly foreign to all our human language. However alien it may be to the conscious awareness of the estranged man, it is surely never alien to his actual existence, for "in him we live and move and have our being." [26]

Finally, we cannot but be somewhat shocked that Thurneysen quotes with such resounding approval the callous advice of Wilhelm Löhe to an individual suffering from severe fantasies: "All these things are partly illness, partly temptation, and like most temptations are pure lie and deceit. The truth is that God in Jesus Christ is merciful unto you. Man against man! My word against yours! " [27] It is slightly short of incredible that such aloof lack of internal participation, such a brazen denial of empathy under the guise of proclamation, could be advised for pastoral care. The argumentative gauntlet "my word against yours! ", in our view, goes diametrically against the best therapeutic practice and the very nature of the healing process which centers in empathetic understanding. It is not my word against his, but rather his own deepest word against some false word in himself, and therefore at a level often far beyond human cognition, God's own Word participating in his struggle for self-fulfillment. It is not my word against his, but God's word present for both of us and in both of us, however inarticulate it may be for both counselor and counselee.

Barth's polemic against natural theology cannot be persuasively directed against a strict " client-centered " type of therapy that does not in any sense propose to speak of *God,* but only to participate radically in the human condition in its inauthenticity and possibility. One might better speak of effective psychotherapy as a dekerygmatized soteriology with an implicit Christology than a *natural theology,* in the strict sense of a theology that intends to speak explicitly of *God* from some analogy with being.

Our intention in part has been to find a reliable theological basis for applying well-tested therapeutic attitudes to the process of pastoral help. If admittedly various types of psychotherapy have been uncritically borrowed by Protestant pastoral care without much serious theological reflection, this need not be so in the future. We have reason to believe that effective therapeutic attitudes can be shown to be implicitly congenial with an adequate Christology and theology of revelation, even when one employs a relentless Barthian critique of natural theology.

Chapter VI

Hiltner's Operation-centered Pastoral Theology

A third position with which I have found myself in creative tension and dialogue is that of Seward Hiltner, whose prolific literary career, including such works as *Pastoral Counseling* and *Preface to Pastoral Theology* and many other books and articles, has been marked with clear insight and a keen eye for the practical problems of the pastor as counselor. Hiltner's contribution has not been so much creative theological reflection as a sensitive understanding of the pastoral situation, and a translation of psychotherapeutic procedures into this context. Though many others of varying stature have been involved in this task, Hiltner is chief among them and has probably done more to teach Protestant pastors helpful therapeutic attitudes than any other individual. He has shown little inclination, however, to follow certain important clues from current Biblical studies, the discussion of hermeneutics, or from the new ecclesiology emerging from the ecumenical lay movement, where much is to be learned about pastoral care. Our discussion intends to show how Hiltner's program lends itself, perhaps better than either Tillich's or Thurneysen's, to continued development in the light of contemporary theology.

1. The Pragmatic Syndrome

A principal strength of Hiltner's discussion over against Thurneysen's is that he is willing to borrow from the wisdom of dynamic psychology and current psychotherapy on behalf of the church's service. Summarily he writes: " In terms of basic attitude, approach and method, pastoral counseling does not differ from effective counseling by other types of counselors. It differs in terms of the setting in which religious counseling is done, the religious resources which are drawn upon, and the dimension at which the pastor must view all human growth and human problems." [1] Surely the reader cannot avoid a basic decision as to whether he wants to buy this point. The helping process functions either essentially the same or essentially differently in pastoral care than it does in ordinary psychotherapy. I wish to make it clear that for my part Hiltner is right, over against both Tillich and Thurneysen, to emphasize the essential consistency of the therapeutic process, whether in a churchly or secular context, and thus the basic similarity of pastoral counseling with other types of counseling, given of course the specific qualifications he makes above. In my view, neither professional psychotherapy nor pastoral care has a monopoly on the therapeutic forces that are inherent in life itself that from time to time may appear in any ordinary interpersonal relationship, but that have recently received more adequate formulation with the development of clinical psychology. It should also be evident that my entire discussion moves against the current of the self-conscious professionalism that so deeply infects psychiatric and psychotherapeutic practice today. At least we can be thankful that the pastoral ministry has largely been spared this phony vocational snobbery, largely borrowed from bourgeois medical practice, which so profoundly debilitates genuine therapeutic effectiveness. Protestant pastoral care can in no sense allow itself to become a partner to a deeper entrenchment of a disdainful professionalism.

Both strength and weakness may be found in Hiltner's simple definition of pastoral counseling as " the attempt by a pastor to help people help themselves through the process of gaining understanding of their inner conflicts." [2] Its strength is its pragmatism. Its weakness is its generality, devoid of theological reference, and its failure (apart from surface methodological criticisms) to apply a deliberate theological critique to the assumptions of the therapeutic process. I wish strongly to affirm the pragmatic accent of American pastoral care, unentangled by the confessional, ideological, and polemical issues that bedevil Continental pastoral care, but not in such an unqualified way as to regard simple pragmatism as sufficient or to neglect the continuing quasi-theological task of pastoral care. This points us toward our first thesis for discussion in relation to Hiltner: *However important may be the concrete application of tested therapeutic attitudes to pastoral care, the theological dialogue with therapy cannot rest content to remain at the instrumental level of pragmatic borrowing or professional cooperation, but must plumb to the depths of the theological assumptions of therapy itself.*

A sharp pragmatic focus is evident from the first pages of *Pastoral Counseling,* where Hiltner wastes no time launching into a discussion of technique, approach, verbatim-interview analysis, etc. Although the first chapter title leads one to believe he is going to discuss the theological " Aims and Assumptions of Pastoral Counseling," he instead dodges any theological prolegomena whatsoever and moves busily into interview analyses. More noteworthy for what they omit than what they include are the two potential beginning points he offers for the study of pastoral counseling: (*a*) an inquiry into psychological dynamics, and (*b*) concrete interview materials analyzing counseling approach and method. He prefers the latter " because it follows John Dewey's general rule that we learn in proportion as we recognize our interests to be touched." [3] It is only fitting that Dewey be quoted from the outset in a discussion which views pastoral counseling essentially as a type of problem solving. An unvarnished pragmatism is likewise revealed in his frank acknowledgment that " all pastors know they have to counsel, and their first question is: How? " [4] This is Hiltner's beginning point.

There is admittedly much to commend such pragmatic

functionalism in its urgent concern for implementing the
helping relationship in a churchly setting, which is perhaps the most significant contribution of recent American
pastoral care. But when this functionalism operates *de
novo,* without an overarching theological framework, it
easily tends toward the uncritical directionless activism so
native to American pragmatism. Demonstrably the American pastoral care movement has drifted along with liberal
theology in general toward antisystematization and even
anti-intellectualism in the sense of resisting deliberately
systematic or theoretical substructures as a basis for its
actual functioning.

We cannot fail to note the telling analogy that Hiltner
draws between cooperation in counseling as similar to an
earlier phase of the ecumenical movement: " Most Protestants have discovered that in the process of common *action* toward objectives which can be better achieved in
co-operation than in separation, they have found vastly
more of a common *faith* than they ever realized they had.
Those who have worked successfully together on counseling are taking the surest road to a similar objective, better
appreciation both of one's own contribution and that of
the other fellow. Theoretical agreement rarely if ever pre-
cedes practical co-operation in a democratic society." And
then, most significantly: " While I have not hesitated to
talk about the equivalent of ' faith and order,' I remain
convinced that the road to ecumenicity in counseling is
' life and work.' " [5] To anyone familiar with ecumenical
conversation of the past thirty years, as Hiltner himself was
as an official of the National Council of Churches, this is a
revealing analogy which in effect says that the rapprochement between pastoral counseling and other forms of therapy may better proceed basically at the level of practical cooperation without facing squarely what may be the
tougher theological and philosophical issues that lie sub-
merged beneath questions of therapeutic approach and
praxis. Just as the ecumenical movement has been forced
to go beyond pragmatic cooperation and comparative ec-

clesiology and face up to hardheaded dialogue on the essential issues of the church's unity and mission, likewise the dialogue with therapy is now being called to go beyond its earlier stages of pragmatic cooperation and comparative anthropology and face up to a serious discussion on the underlying assumptions of our operational processes, assumptions about which we cannot afford to be deceptive or apologetic.[6]

2. THE ECLIPSE OF PROCLAMATION

The axial assumption of all Christian proclamation is that God has made himself known. Christian dialogue is thus not in search for the divine self-disclosure, but exists in response to it.[7] A principal concern of our discussion of kerygma and counseling has been to clarify the appropriate relation between proclaiming the event of God's love and mediating it concretely through an interpersonal relationship. In this connection we now frame our second proposition in relation to Hiltner: *If preaching makes explicit the self-disclosure of the accepting reality implicitly presupposed in the therapeutic process, then it is to the interest of counseling to protect the freedom of proclamation to make clear its own unique witness, without attempting to absorb preaching into a more general approach to eductive counseling or precounseling.* We do not find in Hiltner any visible commitment to maintain this freedom of proclamation. Instead, we find a subtle propensity to reduce preaching to a type of counseling. So as we have pointed to Thurneysen's tendency to reduce pastoral care to proclamation, now we must examine Hiltner's inclination to reduce the act of proclamation to a counseling relationship.

Although Hiltner rightly inveighs against " an imperialist attitude " on the part of one theological discipline toward another, it nevertheless becomes clear that when he discusses preaching " viewed in the light of counseling and precounseling principles," [8] such preaching proceeds in much the same way as eductive counseling. He analyzes

sermons and counseling interviews with the same procedures and applies to them the same criteria. " The point is
that far from there being a fundamental contradiction between preaching and counseling, these two functions
should exhibit the same basic approach." [9]

The concept of *precounseling* has been helpfully expli-
cated by Hiltner as a situation in which the counselor offers help in such a way that it may be as easily refused as
accepted, and incorrect expectations can be explicitly denied.[10] The style of preaching that Hiltner commends,
however, takes on most of the characteristics of the precounseling situation. Although he acknowledges differences between preaching and counseling which he says are
" so obvious as not to require comment," [11] he does not
help his reader to understand just what these differences
are except in the most general terms, leaving the stronger
impression of their basic identity. " In counseling we listen more than we talk. In preaching we talk. But this is a
situational difference, not a fundamental difference of attitude and approach." [12] The ultimate purpose of preaching for Hiltner is not that it announces the deed of God
which discloses the ground of our acceptance, but that it
functions pragmatically to bring people to the point of
" thinking more adequately about their human situation "
in order that they may more readily receive the help they
presumably need in counseling.[13]

If the relation between kerygma and therapeia is as we
have described it, however, then we have reason to believe that good therapy itself has something crucial at
stake in forceful, clear Christian proclamation, and that it
wants nothing more than for preaching to mature, to maintain its own identity, and to fulfill its authentic function
by pointing explicitly to the *event* of divine acceptance
which therapy can only quietly and anticipatively presuppose. Pastoral care therefore has little to gain and much to
lose in the tendency to reduce preaching to a form of counseling.

3. Reversing the Pragmatic Hermeneutic

Closely related to this point is our next proposition, that *Scripture, worship, and doctrine, often used in recent pastoral care in an instrumental fashion as a* deus ex machina *for human suffering, must now be allowed to raise their own questions to pastoral care, thus reversing the hermeneutical circle established by pragmatic activism.*

Perhaps the most disturbing aspect of Hiltner's functional use of theology appears in his discussion of " Religious Resources "[14] for pastoral counseling where he shows how prayer, Scripture, doctrine, and sacrament all have certain instrumental contributions to make to counseling. Bonhoeffer's devastating critique of all stratagems that would use religion as a *deus ex machina,* or problem solver for human troubles, directs itself against such thinking, not only in Hiltner but in a broad spectrum of recent writers in pastoral care.[15]

Although we can hardly quarrel with Hiltner's deeper intention to " make prayer relevant to the spiritual needs found in conditions of stress and tension," [16] such an emphasis can easily lead to a distortion of the essential meaning of prayer as God's own hearing of our petition, confession, and thanksgiving, shifting the focus instead toward our own stratagems of communication with the person with whom one is offering prayer. That Hiltner falls into this distortion is evident when he argues that in prayer the *need* of the person is the essential " point from which to start " [17] rather than the hearing and speaking of God without which prayer is reduced to psychological manipulation.

More disappointing, however, is his pragmatic description of " the *use* of the Bible " [18] in counseling. " The pastor will use the Bible in counseling, as he understands it and as it applies to particular situations with which he is dealing, in the sense of using the truths and doctrines revealed there." [19] The Bible is consulted only when it is useful for solving certain problems framed by the human situation, not to reframe one's understanding of the human situation itself. This is what we mean by a pragmatic hermeneutic.

Even Christian doctrine assumes a functional aspect in relation to pastoral counseling. So latitudinarian is Hiltner's definition of doctrine, however, that one must wonder exactly what he means when he writes: "Apart from certain extreme positions, therefore, what is said [here] should have relevance for nearly all the Christian theological positions widely held in this country." [20] Thus, whatever doctrinal resources there may be for counseling appear to have nothing whatsoever to do with the adequacy, rootage, truth claims, or consistency of the doctrine but merely with the psychological effect of the doctrine on the counselee.

4. LIBERAL PIETISM

The essential direction of Hiltner's theological method, which he calls "operation-centered," is likewise strongly experiential and pragmatic. With single-minded determination, he intends to derive "theological conclusions" (presumably knowledge of God, creation, redemption, etc.) from operational studies, interview materials, and pastoral situations: "What is learned from the study of operations, when approached with theological questions in mind and followed by the drawing of theological conclusions, brings light or knowledge that is theological in character. The movement from operations to conclusions must be regarded as theological." [21] This general viewpoint makes it necessary for us to set forth this last thesis for discussion in relation to Hiltner: *A pragmatic theological method that does not scrupulously protect itself against uncritical cultural absorption and that neglects exegetical and historical issues may find itself painfully unprepared for the style of honest, hardheaded, confessional conversation with the modern healing arts which the current situation demands.* It is my view that a strict application of the *analogia fidei* provides the best available methodological basis for engaging in this sort of conversation with good prospect of gaining a hearing without dilution of the Christian witness.

Hiltner contrasts the study of pastoral theology with all " logic-centered disciplines," or those in which " the key to their distinctive nature lies in a ' logical ' organization of subject matter." [22] It is rather puzzling, however, when Hiltner views the study of the Biblical witness as a "logic-centered " discipline in an era in which Biblical exegesis stands in a determined struggle against arbitrarily structured theological systematization. We are more inclined to characterize recent Biblical study as *event*-centered rather than logic-centered.

Hiltner's alternative to a logic-centered method is an " operation-centered " approach, which argues that theological conclusions are drawn from interpersonal relationships and pastoral experience. If various types of theological methods may be historically distinguished by the relative weight they give to the authority of tradition (Catholic), Scripture (Protestant), reason (rationalist), or experience (pietist), it is clear that for Hiltner as for the whole tradition of pragmatic pastoral care the overwhelming weight of authority for theological knowledge is given to *experience*, and in this sense the American pastoral care movement belongs essentially to the tradition of a liberalizing, pragmatizing pietism. One first *does* certain things and experiences certain relationships, like shepherding the flock, and only then draws valid theological conclusions. The " operation-centered " approach exists where " theological conclusions, or theory or basic principles, emerge from reflection primarily on acts or events or functions from a particular perspective." [23] Hiltner's own view of his most original contribution is that he was able to show how in pastoral care " the theory and approach follow from the study of concrete situations, as demonstrated in interview material." [24] His reliance on verbatim case studies developed as early as 1943 when, under the influence of Rogers, he began to apply case analyses to "students' reports of interviews in church contacts," which according to his own judgment became the central feature of his own best contribution.[25] Although we hardly wish to challenge the validity of interview analysis in pastoral care, we seriously question whether this alone is adequate as a vantage point for drawing theological conclusions without the theological equilibrium that comes from the sustained study of Scripture and tradition and the struggle for rational and systematic self-consistency.

From an entirely different theological commitment we are concerned to show how the more adequate analogy between God's action and the therapeutic process is an analogy of faith that thinks from the self-disclosure of God to human self-disclosure, and not an analogy that proceeds in an allegedly presuppositionless manner first with the study of operations and interview materials and only then draws theological conclusions about the being or action of God. It is for this reason that in our view Hiltner reads the analogy of divine acceptance and therapeutic acceptance exactly backward when in discussing the Pauline view of justification, he proposes that careful scrutiny of therapeutic acceptance "may augment Paul's understanding." [26] The more difficult question of whether Paul's view of justification might conceivably illumine the inner meaning of psychiatric help is never meaningfully raised.

Likewise Hiltner's crucial reliance upon the image of shepherding urgently needs the analogy of faith to place it in clearer focus. So subjective is his definition of shepherding that it finally amounts to little more than "a certain point of view in the subject who is performing the viewing or feeling or helping." [27] Indeed, the shepherd image is, as he says, a prototypical Biblical pattern for pastoral relationships. Actually, however, Hiltner begins with a generalized, untheological conception of shepherding that is derived largely from psychodynamic assumptions and only then reads this already presupposed definition back into the New Testament. The only shepherding of which the New Testament speaks, however, is first of all God's own shepherding of man, and only therefore analogously man's shepherding of his neighbor amid the threats and entanglements of human existence.[28]

PART THREE

THE CONTINUING DIALOGUE

New theological initiatives require a reshaping of the dialogue with psychotherapy. We have examined some of these new initiatives, and compared them with the prevailing patterns available today. Now it is our task to come to grips with some of the more substantial exegetical and systematic issues that cluster around our theme.

Far from being exhaustive, our treatment can only be a brief foray into a very rich area of Biblical, historical, and systematic studies, but several texts and themes demand the most urgent attention. So in the remainder of our discussion we shall limit ourselves to a brief examination of certain paradigmatic New Testament texts that impinge decisively upon our theme, a closer look at the unfulfilled role of Bultmann's theology in the emerging dialogue, and a review of several knotty systematic questions on a theology of the saeculum.

Chapter VII

Exegetical Considerations [1]

Wary of generalized talk of " the Biblical doctrine of " this or that, we keenly sense the need for more careful examination of particular Biblical paradigms and for " textual concreteness " again in our conversation with the Bible.[2] Thus we shall focus on two Biblical texts that have special pertinence for our inquiry, Col., ch. 1, and Matt., ch. 25, and then upon the peculiar pattern of the early church's encounter with gnosticism and its relevance for today's encounter with psychotherapy.

1. Therapy and Cosmos

A single cosmological assumption has undergirded our entire discussion with psychotherapy: that the accepting reality implicit in psychotherapy is rooted in the cosmos itself. Upon what grounds, exegetical or otherwise, do we make this audacious assumption? In answering this, we cannot fail to give careful attention to the expansive cosmic hymn of Col., ch. 1, in which the language of an ancient Hellenistic song of praise is transformed to celebrate the Christ as " the image of the invisible God, the firstborn of all creation; for in him all things were created, in heaven and on earth, visible and invisible, whether thrones or dominions or principalities or authorities — all things [*panta*] were created through him and for him " (Col. 1:15, 16).[3] For in this hymn we find a condensed poetic summary of the witness that appears repeatedly in the

New Testament to the cosmic scope of the therapeutic act of God in Jesus Christ.

If we should find ourselves interested in actually listening to this text, and deeply grasped by it, we find it pressing us much farther than we first expected to go. For all things are alleged to have been created not only *in* Christ, but *through* him and *for* him, or put differently, it is through this redemptive intention and for it that the cosmos itself comes into being, so that the whole panoply of being and time is now known to serve ultimately to reveal the mystery of God's love.[4]

When we come to the New Testament with our human questions, hoping for and expecting direct and (for our purpose) useful answers, we often find the New Testament transforming, revolutionizing, negating, and deepening our questions so as to make them theologically and humanly serious. If we tend to want to dilute the text so as to say that all things are in some sense *addressed* by God, as it were from the outside, the text itself continues to insist that all things are held together, as it were from the inside, by the occurring love of God. If we readily affirm that God in certain moments of *kairos* dramatically touches the world of being, the text instead speaks of the world as having its permanent cement, its cosmic adhesive, its ontological mucilage in the redemptive purpose of God without which it would tend to come unglued. All this is summarized in the simple formula which we take to be the theme of our whole discussion with psychotherapy: *omnia in ipso constant,* " All things in him consist," or as the RSV would have it, " In him all things hold together " (Col. 1:17), i.e., the cosmos has its being in Christ, the welding of its hidden structure is already the love of God, even before the creation of the world.[5]

It is upon this exegetical basis that we have proposed that when the therapist relies upon the healing forces already at work in life itself, when he mediates an acceptance that is not finally his own personal act but a representative ministry on behalf of an acceptance rooted in reality itself, he is thereby implicitly relying upon the very reconciling reality that Christian proclamation explicitly announces as self-disclosed in the Christ event, a reality that remains the hidden cement of the life of the world even when the world exists in estrangement, self-rejection, and ignorance. This hidden structure of grace within the secular dynamism of the world is " the mystery hidden for ages and generations but now made manifest to his saints " (v. 26). The saints are the celebrating community of those who know themselves to have been grasped by the unconditional positive regard of God amid their estrangement. *Now* means the time in which the reign of God has begun and is hastening toward its consummation, in contrast to a (still lingering, but already in process of dying) previous era that has existed in ignorance of the One who holds all things together, an era that attempted to understand itself apart from its hidden matrix of divine *agapē*.[6]

It is through this community and in this time that God has chosen " to make known how great *among the Gentiles* [!] are the riches of the glory of this mystery, which is Christ in you, the hope of glory " (v. 27). It is precisely in the midst of the presumably godless world ("the Gentiles " in their frame of reference, " the secular world " in our frame of reference) that the riches of this mystery are already great, and deserve to be known as great.[7] Thus the purpose of proclamation is " to make the word of God fully known " (v. 25) to those who already stand in it, with the ultimate intention " that we may present every man mature in Christ " (v. 28), i.e., fully aware of who he is. Who is he? One who has been loved by God from the beginning, and whose existence is indefinable apart from the self-disclosure of divine love, whether or not he chooses to celebrate it.[8] For in this event of divine self-disclosure (the constellation of occurrences surrounding the ministry of Jesus of Nazareth) " all the fulness of God was pleased to dwell, and through him to reconcile to himself *all things*, whether on earth or in heaven, making peace by the blood of his cross " (vs. 19, 20). The most inclusive phrase in the cosmology of the first-century man, nothing less than *pas* (all things), "whether on earth or in heaven," emphasizes the scope of the reconciliation now in effect.[9] The peace-making event between being and the ground of being, however, is not remembered by the Christian community merely as an idea in our minds but a concrete occurrence in history with a cross, blood, and innocent death.

2. THE INCOGNITO CHRIST

The last parable of Jesus before his crucifixion (Matt. 25:31-46) impinges powerfully upon our thoughts on the presence of Christ amid the therapeutic process. For it focuses upon the inconspicuous service to the troubled neighbor as a ministry in which Christ himself is a hidden participant. The parable is cast on a cosmic scale: "When the Son of man comes in his glory, and all the angels with him, then he will sit on his glorious throne. Before him will be gathered all the nations, and he will separate them one from another as a shepherd separates the sheep from the goats" (Matt. 25:31, 32). The scene is the Last Day, universally expected in Jewish apocalypticism. The nations are gathered to stand before the final Judge. But what strange sort of judgment awaits them?

The sheep are separated from the goats. The blessed take their place at the right hand of the Messianic King, and the unrighteous are placed on his left hand. Then the criterion, long awaited by human history, is announced to the gathered multitude. It is unexpectedly shocking to the ears of the professionally religious, for it says nothing of piety. It instead focuses directly upon the relation of the Messianic King to the process of charitable, sensitive, helping service (therapeia). The verdict is declared in the form of an invitation to those on the right hand: "Come, O blessed of my Father, inherit the kingdom prepared for you from the foundation of the world; for I was hungry and you gave me food, I was thirsty and you gave me drink, I was a stranger and you welcomed me." A strange court of judgment indeed, and a curious verdict. For the decision of the Judge is expressed in highly personalized terms. It has to do with his own personal relation with the defendant. For *I* was in distress, says the Messianic Judge, and *you* were *my* helper and deliverer! All the more astonishing is this when one fully realizes that the Judge who speaks is himself the expected Deliverer, the Son of Man, anointed of God to bring help to Israel in her darkest hour. It is the Deliverer who speaks of himself in the most improbable manner as having been delivered. It is the King himself who incredibly describes himself as having been imprisoned, estranged from the structures of society. It is the Creator of all things who describes himself unthinkably as without a home, a stranger. It is the Healer of history who speaks of himself as having suffered sickness. What an ironic twist of the story at the last moment of history! In short, the Expected One reveals himself as one who has been living in expectation, looking for help from afar!

The Judge further addresses the inheritors of the Kingdom in the most intimate way: "*I* was naked and you clothed me, I was sick and you visited me, I was in prison and *you* came to me." The blessed in the last days are those who have rendered concrete, sensitive, caring service (therapeia) to the expected Deliverer, the Son of Man, whom they have met in need. They were not ashamed to visit him in prison, they knew of his sickness and took the direct initiative to comfort him, saw his nakedness and clothed him — all simple, direct acts of care, unaware of their ultimate significance, but so impressive as to constitute the single memory and concern of the Messianic King at the end of days.

This fantastic verdict is received, not with joy or compliance, but with sincere confusion and shocked disbelief. Nothing is farther from the imagination or memory of the blessed than the incredible thought that they could have delivered the expected Deliverer, comforted the Comforter, healed the Healer in his sickness, or visited the ul-

timate Friend in his loneliness. Guilelessly, almost argu-
mentatively, they protest the mistaken identity: "Lord,
when did we see thee hungry and feed thee, or thirsty
and give thee drink? And when did we see thee a stranger
and welcome thee, or naked and clothe thee? When did
we see thee sick or in prison and visit thee?" Totally unaware are the righteous of their own righteousness. They
request clarification: *When* did we encounter thee, in all
our worldly encounters?

The answer of the King is still as astonishing and radical
as it is familiar: "Truly, I say to you, as you did it to one
of the least of these my brethren, you did it to me." Mark
well that this does not just mean that the neighbor is
merely analogous to the suffering Christ, but that the
Christ concretely meets us precisely in our actual meeting
with the suffering neighbor. The most immediate and personal relation to the Christ that we have this side of the
Day of Judgment is our immediate and personal relation
to the neighbor in need. "The least of these" refers to
those who share most deeply and inconspicuously in the
estrangement, thirst, and sickness of the world, even as
God himself shares in it. To the extent that we have served
the least of these, we have served Christ. In the measure
we have neglected and despised these, we have neglected
and despised Christ. The text does not mean merely that
we ought to do good deeds in order to receive God's favor,
but that the needy already bear God's favor to us in the
most real sense.[10] Above all, it intends to say that God himself shares radically in our human nakedness, sickness,
bondage, and suffering and calls responsible men and society to alleviate these hurts.

Those who fail to seize the unique opportunity to serve
the needy neighbor, and therefore the hidden Christ, are
viewed in the parable as the "cursed," whose lives have
missed their own deepest intention.[11] In the context of the
mythological world view of the first century, the imagery
used to describe the wretchedness of their situation in the
Last Day is fierce and violent indeed: " Depart from me,

you cursed, into the eternal fire prepared for the devil and his angels; for I was hungry and you gave me no food, I was thirsty and you gave me no drink, I was a stranger and you did not welcome me, naked and you did not clothe me, sick and in prison and you did not visit me." The curse is essentially a *rejection* (Depart from me!) of those who have been personally and willfully responsible for the rejection of the Messianic Judge. The negative verdict is likewise received with disbelief. The unrighteous are the first to claim their righteousness. However much they may have neglected their human brothers in the past, they remember no occasion when they neglected to love and honor God. When they protest, " Lord, when did we see thee hungry or thirsty or a stranger or naked or sick or in prison, and did not minister to thee? " the Messianic reply must be still the same: " As you did it not to one of the least of these, you did it not to me." And they will go away into eternal punishment, but the righteous into eternal life. Does the parable thus mean that God damns those who fail to love? More profoundly, it means that those who fail to love have already chosen in their relation to the neighbor a certain form of self-damnation which misses the possibility for authentic life which is at hand and being offered already in the least of these. What has all this to do with psychotherapy?

Psychotherapy is a process of *welcoming* the stranger — he who is estranged from himself, away from home, wandering in an alien land — into a relationship of trust, care, and mutual respect. Psychotherapy is a process of *visiting* the imprisoned, those chained to their own compulsions, shackled by self-deception, pacing the narrow cells of guilt and anxiety, and talking with them about their prospects for freedom. Psychotherapy is a process of *clothing* the nakedness of those who have been stripped by illness of all pretense and self-respect, whose emptiness and failure have been laid bare to the world, who have been deprived of all protective devices, masks, barriers, and hiding places. Psychotherapy is a special way of *calling* upon and sojourning within the inner frame of reference of those who wait under the conditions of helpless sickness, yearning daily for the day of deliverance. Psychotherapy, when effective, is a *slaking* of the thirst of those who have been deprived of warm, loving care, a *feeding* of those who hunger for understanding, acceptance, and authentic friendship. When it is ineffective, the hunger continues to gnaw, the thirst remains unabated, the nakedness grows ever more ashamed, the prisoner neglected, the stranger unwelcomed, and the strength of the sick increasingly drained by the delay of hope.

Something ultimate, as symbolized in apocalyptic imagery by the Day of Judgment, seems to be at stake in the effectiveness of this service. Something final hinges upon how sensitively the helper functions in this relationship. For it is none other than the final Judge himself, according to the ironic imagery of Jesus, who shares in this suffering, and who finally meets one in the imprisoned neurotic, the naked schizophrenic, and the sick paranoic. Christ himself is the hidden participant in the encounter of the helper and the helped, and in the neglect of the neglected he himself is despised and the relationship is already cursed. Far from comforting the therapist with the pious thought that his service is a service to God, the text actually puts all our therapeutic efforts under the severest judgment, and were it not for the forgiveness of God present amid all our sin and insensitivity, none of us would be called blessed.

3. The Gnostic Dialogue as a Pattern for Psychotherapy

The church, born into a rapidly gnosticizing Judaism, faced from the beginning the supreme dilemma of proclaiming the gospel in an understandable vocabulary to its contemporaries without losing its distinctive identity as the Christ-congregation of the End of Days. Jesus the proclaimer of the new age had become the proclaimed. The proclaiming church, by no means an orthodox unity, spread rapidly and diversely into the Gentile world, announcing the reign of God and preaching Jesus as Lord.[12] But how was this proclamation convincingly to be expressed to Hellenistic ears now in a whirlwind of syncretism and already beginning to be deeply persuaded by the gnostic understanding of man and the world? The answer to this, as it is only now emerging for the first time in the history of Biblical studies through the labors of Bultmann and his critics,[13] is one of the most surprising and memorable stories in the history of the church's dialogue with its contemporaries.

One of the given significant options for self-understanding in the first century, as psychotherapy, existentialism, and Marxism may be considered given options to the twentieth, was an incipient gnosticism, which offered secret, supernaturally bestowed knowledge (gnosis) *necessary for salvation.*[14] Although it was in the constant flux of eclecticism, three consistent characteristics of this *gnosis* may be identified: (*a*) it was a knowledge totally unavailable from within " this world "; (*b*) it was a gift, inaccessible to natural man, often received in an ecstatic vision, and resulting in a new birth; and (*c*) it was a divine power entering into man's body, driving death out of him, setting him free from fate, and giving him authority and superiority over the ignorance of this world.[15]

The gnostic understanding of man and the world developed in sharp opposition to both the Old Testament and classical Greek views, in that it perceived man as utterly estranged from his true being, a foreigner on alien soil, and the world as a great cosmic prison of darkness, hostile to health and reality.[16] For gnosticism, creation was a vast cosmic tragedy. The myth of man's origin tells of how the demonic powers seized and kidnapped certain foolish or fallen splinters of the light-world and took them into this dark world of captivity. Now, having stupefied them with the pleasures of this world, they are drunk and asleep to their heavenly origin.[17]

Amid this predicament some have been given *gnosis* to enable them to understand themselves as particles of the light-person who rules the heavenly world, sometimes called Primal Man. The redemption myth is the drama of how a light-person, the son and image of the most high god, is sent from the light bringing *gnosis*, awakening the sparks of light, reminding them of their true home, and teaching them the password so they can get by the demonic watchmen.[18] The redeemer, who is to show them the Way back to heaven on their journey after death, does not appear in divine form on earth, but remains disguised so as to remain unrecognized by the demonic rulers, taking upon himself the misery of human existence until he is elevated to the world of light.[19]

Although the church, born into a gnosticizing milieu, was from the outset in unavoidable dialogue with this understanding of life, its earliest responses were polemic and rejection. For it quickly sensed in primitive protognosticism a stiff competitor and opponent, as is evident from many polemical New Testament texts. The earliest preaching contrasted itself with gnosticism in these respects: (*a*) Against all polytheistic overtones of syncretistic gnosticism, it strongly asserted the oneness of God. (*b*) Against the gnostic inclination to separate creation and redemption, it proclaimed that the God who gives life to the world is the same as the redeemer who restores it to life when it is fallen. (*c*) It affirmed the body as the good creation of God, against gnostic asceticism. (*d*) It preached the true humanity of Jesus, against the notion of a disguised redeemer who finally remains unhistorical. (*e*) It proclaimed the resurrection of the dead, through which God himself affirms history, against the gnostic view of death as an escape from history.[20]

Later preaching, moving deeper into the Hellenistic orientation, began to see in gnostic cosmology and mythology a legitimate vocabulary for a penetrating expression of the Christian faith. The gnostic myth and its stock of terms were well known to vast numbers of people. So, *while continuing to protest gnosticism in the ways already noted, the church at the same time began to lift the gnostic redeemer-mythology out of its commonly understood framework and inform it with the Christian proclamation.*[21]

Perhaps the most striking manner of presenting the church's restructuring of gnostic cosmology and mythology would be by a two-column comparison, showing some of the gnostic categories, then the New Testament adaptations:

GNOSTIC COSMOLOGY	NEW TESTAMENT PROCLAMATION
Satan as ruler over the world.[22]	Now shall the ruler of this world be cast out. (John 12:31.)
Demonic principalities and powers enforce the separation of man from his heavenly origin.[23]	[Christ] disarmed the principalities and powers and made a public example of them, triumphing over them. (Col. 2:15.)
The struggle of light and darkness determines the destiny of the world.[24]	Once you were darkness, but now you are light in the Lord; walk as children of light. (Eph. 5:8.)
The cosmic struggle is not against historical beings but against spiritual powers in the region of air, the lower sphere of the firmament.[25]	For we are not contending against flesh and blood, but against the principalities, against the powers, against the world rulers of this present darkness, against the spiritual hosts of wickedness in the heavenly places. (Eph. 6:12.)
The state of creation: fallen, decadent, bound, and without hope.[26]	For the creation was subjected to futility, not of its own will but by the will of him who subjected it in hope; because the creation itself will be set free from

its bondage to decay and obtain the glorious liberty of the children of God. (Rom. 8:20, 21.)

GNOSTIC ANTHROPOLOGY

NEW TESTAMENT PROCLAMATION

Man is born into bondage to the evil rulers of the world.[27]

Man is imprisoned in the world, his will controlled and frustrated by the demonic powers, his body dead to the impulses of light.[28]

All men, both Jews and Greeks, are under the power of sin. (Rom. 3:9.) I am carnal, sold under sin. I do not understand my own actions. For I do not do what I want, but I do the very thing I hate. . . . It is no longer I that do it, but sin which dwells within me. . . . Wretched man that I am! Who will deliver me from this body of death? Thanks be to God through Jesus Christ our Lord! (Rom. 7:14-25.)

Created existence is estranged existence; man is not at home in the world, an alien on foreign soil.[29]

So then you are no longer strangers and sojourners, but you are fellow citizens with the saints and members of the household of God. (Eph. 2:19.)

Man is asleep, drunken, unable to remember his heavenly origin, needing to be awakened, sobered.[30]

Awake, O sleeper, and arise from the dead, and Christ shall give you light. (Eph. 5:14.) So then let us not sleep, as others do, but let us keep awake and be sober. (I Thess. 5:6.)

GNOSTIC REDEMPTION MYTHOLOGY

NEW TESTAMENT PROCLAMATION

The primal man, a preexistent divine being, Son of the Father of lights, comes through the framework of the orbits, assumes incognito human form, teaches the *gnosis*, then is exalted back to heaven, having conquered the demonic world rulers, and who by this act is due all glory and honor.[31]

Have this mind among yourselves, which you have in Christ Jesus, who, though he was in the form of God, did not count equality with God a thing to be grasped, but emptied himself, taking the form of a servant, being born in the likeness of men. And being found in human form he humbled himself and became obedient unto death, even death on a cross. Therefore God has highly exalted him and bestowed on him the name which is above every name. (Phil. 2:5-9.)

Primal man, the pioneer-guide to the light source, shows to the elect the *gnosis* of the secret passageways through the orbits, enduring the miseries of earthly existence to save many.[32]

For it was fitting that he, for whom and by whom all things exist, in bringing many sons to glory, should make the pioneer of their salvation perfect through suffering. (Heb. 2:10.)

The password.[33]

Jesus Christ is Lord. (Phil. 2:11.)

Primal man bears the stamp of the eternal, the image of the highest deity, who, although he makes the wretched journey into finitude, never actually becomes flesh.[34]

He is the image of the invisible God, the first-born of all creation. (Col. 1:15.) He reflects the glory of God and bears the very stamp, of his nature, upholding the universe by his word of power. (Heb. 1:3.) The Word became flesh. (John 1:14.)

	NEW TESTAMENT
GNOSTIC ECCLESIOLOGY	PROCLAMATION
Preexistent kinship between redeemer and redeemed.[35]	For those whom he foreknew he also predestined to be conformed to the image of his Son, in order that he might be the first-born among many brethren. (Rom. 8:29.)
The preexistent unity of men of the spirit, after the analogy of the body and head.[36]	For just as the body is one and has many members, and all the members of the body, though many, are one body, so it is with Christ. (I Cor. 12:12.)
The marriage of redeemer and redeemed.[37]	For the husband is the head of the wife as Christ is the head of the church, his body. (Eph. 5:23.)
The primal man gathers the light-splinters into a union and qualifies them to share in the kingdom of light.[38]	The Father . . . has qualified us to share in the inheritance of the saints in light. He has delivered us from the dominion of darkness and transferred us to the kingdom of his beloved Son. (Col. 1:12, 13.)

These are merely a few selected, striking examples of how the early church seized and utilized a prevailing cosmological-mythological structure and pressed it into the service of the proclamation of the Christ event. We introduce this into our dialogue with psychotherapy to illustrate *the radical freedom of the New Testament church to utilize available linguistic frames of reference and (even antagonistic) popular world views for its own distinctive proclamation, while avoiding uncritical absorption by them.*[39]

Since early gnostic teachers " left no literary records of their own, and since their teachings and ceremonies were usually given orally to initiates only under strict vows of secrecy," [40] we have little direct knowledge of the details of protognostic teaching. In fact, our interpretation of the dialogue between Christianity and protognosticism hinges on the probability that protognostic sources were available in oral tradition early in the first century.[41] According to Bultmann, whose views we are essentially following, the most crucial phase of the church's dialogue with protognosticism was the pre-Pauline Hellenistic church, with the basic adaptive patterns taking shape during the A.D. 30's and 40's, before Paul's influence was being broadly felt.[42] If the astute reader wonders why so many Pauline sources are used to document the pre-Pauline development, the answer of course must lie in the attempts of form criticism and tradition history to seek out patterns of earlier oral traditions as expressed by the later written sources.[43] If in any event our only sources for pre-Pauline developments are Pauline and post-Pauline, the task of the student of the oral tradition becomes that of locating prior forms within the available sources. Thus although Johannine, Pauline, Ignatian, and other later sources are used by Bultmann for the documentation of the gnostic-Christian dialogue, it is quite likely that the earliest and most decisive stage of this encounter was the pre-Pauline Hellenistic church in the maelstrom of syncretism.

Thus over a period of several decades, the most crucial of which were the earliest ones, the church made the irreversible decision to use prevailing world views in its proclamation. And it so happened that an eclectic but widely understood gnosticism was, along with Jewish apocalypticism, a prevailing option with a dramatic stock of terms ready for employment. The impact of this choice upon the

subsequent Christian tradition is impossible to underesti-
mate. It was immense, absolutely immense. Because of its
historical priority to all other world views through which
the church subsequently moved, and because the theological resources through which the later church understood
the early church were all unalterably cast in its terminol-
ogy (and until form critical studies indistinguishably
mixed with it), gnostic language has placed its stamp
upon the entire Christian tradition. If gnosticism was,
from the beginning, a competitor and harassment to the
church, a deeper perception might also acknowledge it as
a valuable gift in the fullness of time amid the providential ordering of history.

Having reviewed the essential terms of the primitive
church's decisive and prototypical dialogue with gnosticism, we are now prepared to ask what this means for our
current dialogue with psychotherapy. We propose that
*psychotherapy, psychoanalysis, and psychiatry in some
sense stand in much the same decisive relation to Christian proclamation today as gnosticism did in the first century.* Just as gnosticism was eclectic and diverse, so today
are recent psychotherapeutic theories increasingly multi-
faceted and varied, but nonetheless taken as a whole they
offer a significant option for twentieth-century self-understanding, rivaled perhaps only by Marxism, scientific empiricism, and existentialism. Like gnosticism, modern psychotherapy offers deliverance through *gnosis.* Like
gnosticism, psychotherapy views the human predicament
under the analogy of a radical imprisonment to unseen
(unconscious) and demonic (self-destructive) powers that
have taken hold of man's volition and delivered his body
over to death.[44] Just as in gnosticism man's problem is that
he has irretrievably forgotten who he is and his salvation
is a process of breaking down resistances and breaking
through to a new memory, so in psychotherapy the man in
trouble has so completely forgotten or misplaced his identity that he needs help to " find himself again " through a

process of anamnesis, and must renegotiate the wrong turns in his past traumas.[45]

We do not so much propose that psychotherapy is a new form of gnosticism (although other parallels could be noted) but that the overall predominating status of psychotherapy as a prevailing quasi-religious twentieth-century option with viable proposals for the solution of the human predicament of anxiety, guilt, and bondage places it in much the same position that the early church found the gnostic movement occupying. As gnosticism was in the process of eroding away the vulnerable structures of introverted Judaism, so today is psychotherapy in the process of eroding away the deteriorating structures of Western bourgeois morality that have for so long been identified with the Protestant ethic.[46] As in its encounter with gnosticism, the church today finds itself standing very ambivalently before psychotherapy, on the one hand in tension with its reductive naturalism, and on the other hand attracted and impressed by the depth of its understanding of sickness and healing.[47] Above all, however, psychotherapy, like gnosticism, offers to Christian proclamation a large stock of terms in wide usage by men of the twentieth century which can be pressed to the service of the Christian witness. The danger, of course, is that in the process of appropriating the authentic wisdom of its partner in dialogue, the church may lapse into mere uncritical cultural absorption, so that its distinctive witness is eclipsed and it appears to the world as merely another form of psychologism.

CHAPTER VIII

Bultmann and the Ontology of Acceptance

It is regrettable that the one Biblical exegete whose whole theological effort most powerfully lends itself to dialogue with psychotherapy has never seriously pursued that dialogue — namely, Rudolf Bultmann. Since I am convinced that his theological program has a great and unfulfilled contribution to make to this discussion, I shall examine certain clear themes in Bultmann's theology, especially his penetrating interchange with existential philosophy, which provide some reliable clues as to what we might expect from a post-Bultmannian engagement with current psychotherapy. My own argument will appear in a series of theses that emerge in relation to Bultmann's circumspect discussion of natural theology.

1. CONCEPTUALIZING AND ACTUALIZING AUTHENTICITY

The line Bultmann draws between philosophy and kerygma hinges upon a crucial distinction between possibility in principal and possibility in fact. He argues that authenticity may be adequately conceptualized by existential analysis as a formal ontological possibility in principle, but is actualizable as an ontic possibility in fact only under the address of the Christian proclamation.[1] We now ask whether this may help clarify the appropriate distinction between the health toward which psychotherapy aims and the life of Christian faith and obedience. The astute reader, in fact, may have felt that I have tended uncritically to equate the psychotherapeutic process with the

Christian proclamation, or to absorb one into the other. This discussion vis-à-vis Bultmann will now give me an opportunity to clarify how they may be properly distinguished, hopefully without falling into a "thinking in terms of two spheres."

The ground upon which I have defended Bultmann's curious distinction between possibility in principle and possibility in fact is that he is linguistically correct and internally self-consistent to argue that one can conceive of a genuine possibility for self-fulfillment which he cannot under the circumstances (of sin) actualize.[2] The deeper issue here, however, is whether authentic existence is, after all, fully and adequately conceptualizable either through *Daseinsanalysis* or psychotherapy. I am inclined to think *not* with complete adequacy by either, although there may be many ways in which they partially and approximately grasp authenticity in a formal sense, or envision in a fragmented way the authentic character of self-fulfillment in freedom. But that which Bultmann claims for *Daseinsanalysis*, we must claim even more urgently for psychotherapy: *Healthy authenticity can be conceptualized, and has been, with real, though incomplete, adequacy by contemporary theories of therapy.* One might take as an example the rich construct of the full-functioning person, which describes the dynamics of freedom from guilt, openness to experience, self-acceptance, responsible love for the neighbor, etc., all without any language about God.[3] It is a picture that Christian theology cannot fail to admire and cannot deny without denying itself.

Bultmann just as strongly insists, however, that although existential analysis can conceptualize such authenticity, actualizing it is quite another matter. For freedom and love can be fully realized only in response to a concrete relationship in which one has been unconditionally loved and freed to respond to life with complete openness toward the future. Only the event of divine unconditional love can finally enable such a response, according to Bultmann.[4] But can a similar distinction apply to psychotherapy? In part, yes, for however adequately theories of therapy may describe the construct of the full-functioning person, actually being loved in an event wherein one can know himself to be unconditionally valued, and thus freed for authenticity, is an entirely different matter.[5] But this is just the point at which the process of effective psychotherapy becomes an embarrassment to Bultmann's thesis, for *psychotherapy not only theoretically conceptualizes authenticity, it goes about the practical process of actualizing it, of enabling it, of embodying it!* It attempts to free the individual through ostensibly secular and humanistic means to live life authentically. From time to time it is remarkably successful. Furthermore, its description of human maturity and full-functioning is not a speculative theory of authenticity, but is, in fact, derived strictly from clinical descriptions of effective treatment. Thus the distinction Bultmann makes between existential analysis and kerygma cannot be properly applied to kerygma and psychotherapy. For psychotherapy is not primarily concerned with conceptualizing authenticity as an ontological possibility, but with mediating a relationship of accepting love that will *in fact* free one for authenticity.[6]

Admittedly, I am pursuing a risky course in the sense of not being able to anticipate all its consequences, but I am, nevertheless, compelled by the persuasiveness of clinical evidence to pursue it to the end. The essential proposal of my entire project, as it has been earlier formulated in *Kerygma and Counseling*, is that *the accepting reality, which is implicitly presupposed in effective psychotherapy, is explicitly celebrated as event in the Christian kerygma.*[7] We may even speak circumspectly of the effective psychotherapeutic process, and other relationships in which unconditional positive regard enables authenticity, as the incognito embodiment of Christ. But is not such talk mere double-talk, of a "taking form," but "in disguise"? Not if we buy with full seriousness Bonhoeffer's exegesis on the "taking form" of Christ in worldly contexts, which has its roots in Colossians, Ephesians, Galatians, and Corinthians. It is not for nothing that the Gospel of Matthew declares that "God is able from these stones to raise up children to Abraham" (Matt. 3:9).

But now, are we going to get ourselves into the soteriological trap of admitting that psychotherapy can not only conceptualize but also actualize authenticity in fact? Such an admission, assuming that the Christian life also means an authentic life, might undercut any claim of uniqueness for the Christian message. Again with Bultmann, we stop short of such reductionism.[8] On the one hand, it seems clear that effective psychotherapy achieves many fragmented forms of authenticity: Men are actually being freed from despair and guilt, and freed for hope, trust, love of the neighbor, etc. These things actually happen in psychotherapy every day. On the other hand, we insist with equal emphasis that the therapeutic process is never finally understandable from a naturalistic perspective, but that it *de facto* operates only by rooting itself concretely in the accepting reality of *deus pro nobis,* however little it may know of the event in which divine love is finally known and dramatized in such a way that it is fully knowable. To use more traditional symbols, God the Holy Spirit acts to enable the natural man through prevenient grace frailly to embody and brokenly to reflect his own forgiving love, which is only finally clarified in the Christ event. Therefore, Christian worship celebrates an event of divine action, through which, by analogy, the action of the human helper is made understandable and given historical rootage.

Although, in his essay on hermeneutics, Bultmann argues that " an *existentiell* knowledge about God is alive in the form of the inquiry about ' happiness,' ' salvation,' the meaning of the world and history, and the inquiry into the real nature of each person's particular ' being,' " [9] it becomes clearer in his discussion of natural theology that such knowledge is not, properly speaking, knowledge of God, but merely man's knowledge of the terminus of his striving.[10] All men possess such knowledge of their limitation. Although faith acknowledges this limit as the hidden God, for unfaith such knowledge amounts only to a negative knowledge of the absence of God.[11] Bultmann wisely disclaims any knowledge of God or "point of contact" apart from God's own self-disclosure. The faith that has an eye for the efficacious activity of God in secular processes where the divine presence is totally unrecognized, however, has good precedent as early as the eighth-century prophets. *We, therefore, claim for psychotherapy what Bultmann claims for existential analysis, that it reveals man, perhaps even better than existential philosophy, as a being under moral and noetic limitation, and in that limited and special sense it may know God, via negativa, as that unknown power that stands at the terminus of human striving, caring, longing, and knowing.*[12] The more difficult task, however, is to clarify the sense in which faith sees in secular processes what they do not see in themselves, without distorting the process or imposing upon it something quite alien to its intent. Again, we must wonder whether Bultmann is wise to place such emphasis upon knowledge of God only on the *boundary*, at the edge of the human situation, in striking contrast to Bonhoeffer who calls us always to celebrate God at the *center* of human life.

In reacting against the overemphasis of kerygmatic theology upon faith as the precondition for knowledge of God's action, Wolfhart Pannenberg has boldly argued that the action of God stands "open to everyone who has eyes to see," that he who does not see it is merely "blind," that genuine faith is awakened by "uninhibited observation," and that, "it is not by any means necessary to bring faith already with us in order to find in the history of Israel and of Jesus the revelation of God."[13] The concept of faith against which Pannenberg's polemic is directed, however, as faith which presumably "comes before" revelation, is surely not the faith of which the New Testament speaks, nor of kerygmatic theology as we know it, except at its worst. If faith exists only in response to revelation, one does not first have faith in order to see, but rather, one's faith is a response to a certain kind of seeing, not a seeing which exists on its own initiative but which understands itself as having been seen and known by God. But if it is made clear that faith is a response to an event which is only meaningful in the full sense to those who respond to it, and if faith means precisely that response which sees what otherwise might be neglected in man's ordinary view (God's action), then we can incorporate the deeper intention of Pannenberg's critique into our own stance in kerygmatic theology. In any event, it is clear that for Bultmann, the only "knowledge of God" available to natural man, caught in the syndrome of self-assertiveness and apart from God's own self-disclosure, is merely a knowledge of his own limitation, and thus only of the *deus absconditus* who stands at the terminus of human knowing and doing, and not proper knowledge of the revealed God.[14]

2. THE LIMITS OF "DASEINSANALYSIS"

The kerygma, however, takes up exactly at the point where existential analysis, according to Bultmann, fails: "This then is the decisive thing which distinguishes the New Testament from philosophy and the Christian faith from a 'natural' understanding of existence: the New Testament speaks about and the Christian faith knows about a deed of God which first makes possible man's self-surrender (*Hingabe*), his faith, his love — in short, his authentic life."[15] Similarly, the decisive difference between kerygma and psychotherapy is that the kerygma speaks of the deed of God, which once for all makes historically concrete the ontological basis for psychotherapeutic acceptance. We intend, however, to say something much more positive about the therapeutic process itself than Bultmann allows for *Daseinsanalysis*, namely, that when effective, it may embody an interpersonal process in which the love that is made known in Jesus Christ is inconspicuously taking shape in history. Using Bonhoeffer's language, it may be viewed as an arena of Christ's worldly formation.

In this connection we cannot fail to note the remarkable similarity between Bultmann's authenticity and Rogers' construct of full-functioning. Both embody the abandonment of fixed security patterns, detachment from idolatrous reliances, release from the past, openness to the future, and radical obedience to the demand of the moment. Thus, *whereas Bultmann uses Heidegger's concept of authenticity to frame the question of natural revelation, we are, instead, employing the therapeutic construct of full-functioning to frame the question of Christ's worldly formation.* The tougher issue now becomes: If we have a reliable concept of full-functioning that describes authentic human existence and can be in some real sense actualized in therapy, do we seriously need the kerygma? Is it not merely excess baggage? Does not all talk of a " once for all deed of God " remain a burdensome remnant of mythology if it cannot be reduced to this-worldly language (Buri, Ogden, Braun)? [16] Bultmann rightly insists that we have not come to grips with Christian faith in our time if we evade this issue. The crux of the matter: " Can we have a Christian understanding of Being without Christ? " [17]

In answer to this delicate question, Bultmann suggests that it might at first seem possible " to have a Christian understanding of Being without Christ, as though what we had in the New Testament was first the discovery and the more or less clear expression, in the guise of mythology, of an understanding of Being which is at bottom man's natural understanding of his Being." [18] To support this view, he cites Jaspers, Kamlah, and Yorck, and he could easily have added many others in psychology who propose precisely this. Heidegger, of course, remains Bultmann's preeminent example of an understanding of being which in many ways " would seem to be no more than a secularized, philosophical version of the New Testament view of human life." [19] If Bultmann's perplexity with Heidegger is serious enough, it is compounded even more gravely when we deal with effective therapists, who are not only saying much the same thing as the New Testament about authenticity, and apparently saying it quite independently, but also are enabling such authenticity to emerge concretely in clinical relationships! Of course, it is debatable as to whether either Heidegger or the therapists are thinking " independently " of the Christian tradition, given the complex historical interaction of Christianity and Western humanism (even atheism).[20] But it is clear that if full-functioning is achievable allegedly " without revelation," then it would seem that the very *raison d'être* of the kerygma is outmoded. But it is precisely the problematic phrase " without revelation " that we would call radically into question, even amid a secular setting in which there is no language whatsoever about God's deed.

The key issue is whether it might be the case that what the New Testament means by the Christian life is actually " the ' natural ' disposition of man." [21] Therapists such as Maslow, Horney, and Rogers have clinical reason to believe that a " self-actualizing tendency " may be seen in even the most regressive neuroses, and that therapy must and can rely upon man's unquenchable impulse toward health. Bultmann circumspectly answers his own question with a very perceptive yes and no, which deserves our careful attention. First, *yes,* because faith is not an alien law heteronomously imposed upon man, but consonant with his created being and his deepest intention. " By faith man enters upon the life for which he was originally created." [22]

At a subtler level, however, we must with Bultmann answer *no,* that faith is not the natural disposition of man as sinner. For *the authenticity that can at least partially be conceptualized by existential analysis, and at least partially actualized by effective psychotherapy, can never be fully actualized, and, therefore, never fully conceptualized, except in response to a relationship in which one is loved, known, and understood by one in whom mistrust is impossible.* Such a relationship is only fragmentarily enacted in therapy, where one is always dealing with a finite hu-

man brother in whom mistrust is always possible. Such a
relationship can be possible only if God's own love is
made known in history.[23] Only the God who has made himself known as utterly trustworthy is utterly trustable.

Although to this point we have been able to extrapolate
Bultmann's distinction between philosophy and kerygma
in the direction of therapy, here the chain of argument
weakens, and it is just here that we believe another direction must be taken. For while Bultmann rightly contends
that the philosophical tradition has been " convinced that
all we need is to be told about the ' nature ' of man in order to realize it," [24] such an illusion is not prominently
found among therapists, who, for the most part, have little
interest in talking about man's " nature " at all. They would
hardly imagine that all one needs to achieve full-functioning is to have it properly described or clearly conceptualized. So, *when Bultmann argues, against the optimism of
philosophy, that it is precisely man's self-assertiveness
which blinds him to the fact of his self-assertiveness, he is
not saying anything different from what is amply demonstrated in therapy every day.* For there are many forms of
inauthenticity that man fails to perceive in himself because to perceive them would already be to give up the illusion of one's self-idealizations (Horney).[25] Thus, when-
ever experiences are subceived as incongruent with the
already inauthentic self-structure, the organism responds
by denying the experience to awareness (Rogers).[26] It is
the very hallmark of inauthenticity that one fails to see
his own inauthenticity. This is not only, as Bultmann says,
" the clearest proof that he is a fallen being," [27] but also
the very heart of the dynamics of neurotic resistance
(Freud).[28] So, as therapists have long known, it does little good merely to tell the depressed individual about his
diagnosis. What he needs is a relationship in which he is
freed to understand and choose himself anew, not merely
an analysis of his predicament. It is only when the self-
deceived man finds himself in the presence of a congruent and empathetic neighbor, who mediates the uncondi-

tional positive regard rooted in reality itself, that it becomes in some sense actually possible for him to perceive more clearly his radical alienation from himself and others. Of course, he "knows" this in the Sartrian sense of bad faith, but does not choose to bring it to conscious awareness.[29] So when Bultmann contends that the New Testament parts company with existential philosophy on the issue of the radical fallenness of man, we are not sure that it thereby parts company with psychotherapy on the same basis. There can be no doubt that the New Testament addresses man as one who is " through and through a self-assertive rebel who knows from bitter experience that the life he actually lives is not his authentic life, and that he is totally incapable of achieving that life by his own efforts." [30] But good therapy is also alert to the recalcitrant resistance of man to awareness of authenticity, and the impotence of the incongruent man to bring his deepest intention into awareness and actualization.

A choosable possibility for authentic life, according to Bultmann, is offered only when the " love of God meets man as a power which embraces and sustains him even in his fallen, self-assertive state. Such a love treats man as if he were other than he is. By so doing, love frees man from himself as he is." [31] Analogous dynamics can be seen in the therapeutic process in this way: Unconditional positive regard accepts man precisely amid his inauthenticity. Although it empathizes with man just as he is, there is a sense in which it deals with man as if he were other than he is, for the therapist refuses to value the depressed or guilt-ridden individual exclusively as he values himself. He values him finally as he is valued by the accepting reality in life itself. It is in the process of valuing him as he is valued " in reality " that he becomes free to value himself and others.

But could the unconditional positive regard of the effective therapist have its basis not merely in the private sympathy and initiative of the therapist but in the heart of reality itself? Is it conceivable that the source of all un-

conditional acceptance might have made itself known in
an event? " It is the claim of the New Testament that this
is exactly what has happened." [32] If this claim is true, then
*the ontology of acceptance, so crucial to therapy yet so
widely ignored by therapists, has its surest foundation in
history in the event of divine love.*

CHAPTER IX

Worldly Theology and Psychotherapy

Having explored some of the exegetical issues surrounding our theme, we must not neglect certain of the more substantial systematic and ethical issues. So in this final chapter we shall examine the case for worldly theology, the prospects for a universalistic Christological humanism, the stickly question of charging fees for psychotherapeutic service, selected contributions of recent systematicians on the question of analogy, and finally the question of why psychotherapy lays a special claim upon theological attention and imagination.

1. THE CASE FOR WORLDLY THEOLOGY

A new style of life is emerging, a new mutation in human existence. We are living in a new age. The new breed of man is radically secularized, immersed in the structures and dynamics of urbanizing, technologizing, postmodern existence. The chief god in his demythologized pantheon is Novelty. Religion is past. The future belongs to man. The gods of religion are only of incidental historical interest. Man lives wholly in this world. For him the thoughts of God and the gods, metaphysics, transcendence, and the supernatural are all quite odd and foreign. Both religion and antireligion, theism and atheism, are issues of the past. He knows what he sees. The world is home. If many of his contemporaries do not share in his style of life, he nevertheless knows that he is a new breed, and senses the wind of history. He doesn't bother trying to convert what history ultimately will convert through death and revolution.

This is the man to whom contemporary theology speaks and will continue increasingly to speak. With roots deep in history and nourished by the Biblical witness, the Christian community is called to bear fresh fruit in this new season. Theology today must be worldly theology, without ceasing to be churchly theology. The task of theology in our era is to live fully sharing in the worldly ethos of this time, alert to what God is doing in this secular context, how God is addressing us through fresh new secular forms, how his word is being spoken by strange lips.

To speak at all of worldly theology is already to open the door to a certain grave misunderstanding which we would hope from the outset to avoid. Whereas to the mind of pietism, "worldly" theology suggests a liberalizing dilution, a wholesale sellout of the Christian faith to the presuppositions of secularism, we are instead treating the process of secularization as the very speech of God in a history that is sadly unable to celebrate his speech. Whereas to the mind of scientism, worldly "theology" suggests a curious anomaly, the paradox of trying to speak of God in a world that has disowned him, we intend to speak of a world that can only fruitlessly try to disown the One who creates, judges, and reclaims it ever anew. If to others a "worldly theology" suggests a world that could be understood through itself, abstractly, apart from its being understood before God, we are compelled to speak only of a world whose being known by God is always already a given in the Christ event. All such pietistic, scientistic, and abstract ideas of worldliness are precisely what we reject on behalf of the celebration of the concreteness of God's involvement in secularizing history. The only worldliness of which we speak is the worldliness in which God himself has chosen to share in the act of creation and the event of redemption.

To speak of worldly theology in our time is to speak preeminently of Bonhoeffer and Teilhard, both of whom were deeply engaged in the secular order, and yet who understood this secular engagement from within the context of the divine milieu. If in previous times such a viewpoint has been expressed through such widely varying traditions as the Psalms, the Johannine literature, Irenaeus, and Calvin, it has been most powerfully grasped in our time in the autobiographical writings of Father Teilhard and Pastor Bonhoeffer. If we take them as our keys to the modern situation, then it surely must be clear that a theology which is most deeply engaged in the world is thereby no less churchly in its commitment and rootage. Both of them were resolutely *church* theologians whose whole understanding of the world emerged within the life of the eucharistic community, and whose personal biographies are to be understood only within the context of radical Christian commitment. The church's mission, accordingly, is to help these secular processes understand themselves in deeper theological dimension, and to celebrate the divine matrix in which they exist.

2. THE COSMIC SCOPE OF THE CHRIST EVENT

The worldly implications of God's love would not come as such a surprise to us were it not for the strong pietistic predisposition which has taught us that God acts essentially within the church and not in the world, that he is present essentially in the converted community but not among the ungodly. If we are now in the process of unlearning what this pietistic assumption has taught us, we must in the future learn to listen anew to the Biblical affirmation that Christ is not only present in the world but the giver of its unity and meaning, that the healing processes at work in the world have their source and basis in him, and that he is the center of the circumference of which psychotherapy is a part.[1]

When Paul, in the climax to his first letter to Corinth, is delivering to his brethren there what he considers of " first importance " in the tradition he has received, he formulates a compact summary of a universalistic Christological humanism: " For as in Adam *all* die, so also in Christ shall *all* be made alive " (I Cor. 15:22). The totality of human history participates already in a juridical and anticipatory sense, in the Christ event. It is the secular world that already stands " in Christ." " All " (*pantes*) simply cannot be translated " some." [2] All are made alive. To say that humanity is already dead in Adam and alive in Christ is not to theorize about a bare possibility, but to point to a here and now actuality. That this formulation is not an incidental statement in Paul, but crucial to his whole intention, is seen in the prominence that it also receives in his letter to the Romans, again in the climactic fifth chapter, where he concludes: " Then as one man's trespass led to condemnation for *all* men, so one man's act of righteousness leads to acquittal and life for *all* men " (Rom. 5:18).[3] It is necessary for us to underscore " *all* " because of our strong pietistic predisposition to read the text in a diluted sense as referring only to the converted community. Note carefully that the text does not say that although Christ's death is *intended* for all men, it is effectual as a verdict of righteousness only for some (those who believe). Instead, it says that Christ's act of righteousness leads to the actual (not potential) verdict of acquittal for *all* men before God. Even as the trespass does not lead merely to a possible, but to an actual and finalized, verdict of condemnation, so does the one man's act of righteousness lead to an actual and finalized verdict of acquittal for all.[4] This is our exegetical basis for viewing the setting of unconditional acceptance in effective psychotherapy as a radical verdict which is finally rendered not merely by the believing or disbelieving therapist but primordially by God himself, and not only toward the individual but finally toward the whole of human history.

The power of Pauline rhetoric is pressed to the service of the same theme in II Corinthians: " For the love of Christ controls us, because we are convinced that one has died for all; therefore all have died. And he died for all, that those who live might live no longer for themselves but for him who for their sake died and was raised " (II Cor. 5:14, 15). One focal idea illuminates and guides all our thinking about man. The old era of his history (Adam for short) is hastening toward destruction. Before God, he is already being viewed as a new creation. Since God regards us from a new point of view in Christ, we are called to view ourselves and others anew. The result is a revolution in human perspective: " From now on, therefore, we regard no one from a human point of view; even though we once regarded Christ from a human point of view, we regard him thus no longer." Thus emerges a universalistic Christological humanism.[5] For if all men are already participants in Christ's death and resurrection, they deserve to be understood, viewed, and honored as such. The scales from our eyes are lifted. We are free to treat them as who they in fact (before God) *are!* Likewise, it is unthinkable that we could any longer view such intimate interpersonal processes as psychotherapy " from a human point of view," i.e., as if the Christ event had never occurred, as if the troubled neighbor were not already, from God's point of view, a new man in Christ with a final verdict already rendered upon his guilt.[6]

A further clarification ensues: "That is, God was in Christ reconciling the world (*kosmos*) to himself, not counting their trespasses against them, and entrusting to us the message (*kērygma*) of reconciliation" (II Cor. 5:19). It is not the church only, but the *kosmos* which is the object of God's love.[7] This holy worldliness is best seen as embodied in the ministry of Jesus, who, when asked by the professionally religious why he mixed with worldly people, answered wryly: "Those who are well have no need of a physician, but those who are sick" (Matt. 9:12). So the incarnate love of God freely moves within the context of human brokenness without itself being broken in order that it may call that brokenness back to its original unity with God.

3. FEES AND VOCATION

In his essay on " Therapeutic Insight Through Transference," psychoanalytically oriented André Godin, S.J., chides me for having neglected, in my phenomenological reflections, the fact that the client pays *money* to the therapist for his service, which to Professor Godin suggests more a satanic possibility than some analogy to God's action.[8] Admittedly this is an issue which should be squarely faced, and one with which I have not dealt.

The problem is: I have elaborated a rather volatile analogy which may even embarrass modest therapists, in which I point out the correspondence between their function and the unconditional loving, accepting, reconciling action of God! Whether aware of it or not, the effective therapist allegedly functions as *participatio Christi!* From this exalted analogy, we now turn our gaze to the ordinary therapist doing his routine daily work, often charging about a dollar a minute for his (suffering!) service and spending his winters in Bermuda. For him it may be just a job, a rather lively livelihood, and he does not care to reflect much on its theological implications. How can the hiatus between this picture and my theological analogy be explained or defended?

We must respond in terms of a broader Protestant doctrine of vocation.[9] We encounter in the vocational sphere a broad, unlegalistic process of giving and receiving of goods and services through which my neighbor serves me and I serve him regardless of motivations and often in spite of bad motivations. Wherever the neighbor is served, whether for gain or self-adulation, whether through one's ordinary vocational activity or in special deeds of care, God is being honored and his great command obliquely obeyed, even if unconsciously.[10] Thus the unskilled laborer who works on the sewer line outside my office window, e.g., not only renders me and my colleagues a valuable (seemingly indispensable) service, but also thereby unknowingly honors God *through* his digging of that ditch in order that we clean-hands people will receive the benefit of plumbing without which our lives would be disordered. There is a sense in which every lawful and legitimate vocation is a service to the neighbor and thus an honoring of God. In fact, a good case can be made for the proposition that there is no conceivable vocation in which some service is not rendered to the neighbor, for how else could a person remain " in business " without giving some service, however distorted or poorly executed. Furthermore, since there can be no efficient exchange of goods and services without money, the receipt of just payment for competent service is, according to good Protestant precedent, a part of the providential ordering of God, however inevitably distorted by sin.[11]

We see the question of the payment of fees for professional psychotherapeutic help within this context, for here a very special act of vocational service is being rendered to urgently troubled and deeply suffering neighbors, an act that occasionally takes on the aspect of embodying the very essence of authentic vocational service: the mediation of reconciling love to others in real need in response to the reality of God's own accepting love. Easily overlooked, of course, is the fact that the therapist himself also needs the ditchdigger, the plumber, the trucker, the scrubwoman, the merchandiser, for his self-fulfillment. But persons in these vocations also from time to time need medical specialists and trained counselors who will help free them from neurotic conflicts. So the therapist renders that service and is paid for it, like any other professional service. The money he receives may or may not be a just payment for the service. He may be like an incompetent plumber who is called to plug a leaky pipe, does not fix it, but is paid anyway. This simply means he is a bad therapist and does not therefore exemplify adequately the helping process that we are here trying to understand.

In the process of effective therapy, however, the helper learns something which from the theological viewpoint is crucial: Insofar as he is effective, he mediates an accept-

ing reality present in life itself, he embodies the offer of
a relationship which says, "You are loved despite your
lovelessness." If this mediation is not present, the therapeutic process does not fully achieve what it promises.
Christian worship celebrates the self-disclosure in history
of the accepting reality which the therapeutic process anticipatively and as a matter of faith presupposes. Our point
is scandalous: He may assess exorbitant fees, and be motivated by self-adulation, narcissistic pride and profit, *but*
to the extent that he is actually effective as a therapist so
that through his empathy and congruence the power of
neurotic compulsion is actually broken, he becomes un-
wittingly an oblique participant in the mediation of God's
own healing love. "We have this treasure in earthen ves-
sels," Paul writes, "to show that the transcendent power
belongs to God and not to us" (II Cor. 4:7). Or to make
the same point in a slightly less scandalous fashion, if the
ditchdigger has on his mind only the banal prospect of
getting his paycheck after a sweaty week of work and then
getting drunk on Saturday night, that does not change one
whit the objective fact that he digs the ditch, renders the
urgently needed service, and thereby participates in God's
design through his common act of labor, however he may
be unaware of it.

Inevitably the therapist will always bring mixed motivations to the relationship, since he himself is a person
with needs. But it is doubtful that he can function even
with much pragmatic effectiveness if his own hungers for
love, money, and esteem become too overweening. Christian proclamation hopes to help men become increasingly aware of the service which God himself has rendered to humanity, and thus the appropriate basis for
understanding our fragmented human services rendered
to our neighbors. But the Christian tradition has long celebrated the providence of God which turns even the wrath
of men to his praising, takes the self-assertive striving
which only unconsciously serves the neighbor and recasts
it into a hymn to the glory of God, even though this glori-

fication is not known by the glorifier.[12] So it is with basely motivated, but nonetheless effective, psychotherapy.

4. Pursuing the Analogy

It is unfortunate that Albert Outler's perceptive discussion of *Psychotherapy and the Christian Message* has chosen the language of diplomacy (alliance, rivalry, etc.) to discuss the relation of therapy and theology, since this language lends itself easily to thinking of the issue " in terms of two spheres," two territories, with rival claims to a disputed no-man's-land. But a deeper perception of the intention of his proposed " alliance " will reveal that it is not inconsistent with our own, and that in Outler we find a reliable foundation upon which to continue building. Outler's discussion must be understood in the context of its postwar historical situation in which a prevailing absorptive theologically uncritical cultural Protestantism threatened to make of psychotherapy a new messianism. He astutely showed how the tradition of psychotherapy had been decisively dependent upon certain philosophical assumptions uncritically borrowed from reductive naturalism.[13]

Outler's " basic proposal for the alliance between psychotherapy and Christianity " is that " while the *practical* wisdom of psychotherapy is a valid resource for the Christian care of souls, its humanist and naturalist *perspective* must be rejected." [14] While I fully concur with his insistence that Christian theology may " gratefully receive the best psychotherapy has to offer, in clinical help and practical wisdom . . . but . . . must stand firm on Christian ground, and not be overly impressed by claims that the *faith* of psychotherapy has the same scientific authority as its clinical axioms," [15] I would wish instead to inquire precisely into the *faith* implicitly presupposed in effective psychotherapy and ask how it is related to the explicit announcement of the kerygma.

In an earlier discussion on *Psychotherapy and a Christian View of Man*, David E. Roberts had examined the "remarkable parallel between the Pauline-Augustinian conception of original sin and the psycho-analytic conception of neurosis." [16] His work was especially useful in its historical nexus for clarifying the promise of practical co-operation between Christianity and psychotherapy from a deeper theological perspective than his predecessors. If Roberts' contribution aimed at showing "that some of the basic concepts of psychotherapy are correlative with the human side of events which Christian doctrine interprets," [17] our effort is instead directed toward showing how the event of divine self-disclosure which Christian doctrine interprets may be correlated through the *analogia fidei* with certain basic operational concepts of psychotherapy. So the thrust of my discussion is complementary and in a sense opposite to Roberts' effort, although not in opposition to his intent, particularly as it is seen in its historical context.

Among recent writers on the relation between psychology and theology, none has been more keenly interested in the question of analogy than Daniel Day Williams, whose book on *The Minister and the Care of Souls* examines the potential analogy between salvation as understood in the Christian community and the healing process in psychotherapy. With Tillich he notes the close linguistic relationship between salvation and health, and that God's saving deed is "itself a kind of healing" of human estrangement.[18] Nonetheless "we cannot identify therapy for specific ills with salvation for the human spirit," since "salvation must transcend all particular therapies." [19] Although much is to be learned from this astute discussion, my own viewpoint diverges from Williams' at two decisive points:

a. Whereas Williams proposes "that the fundamental connection of salvation and therapy is found in the nature of *man*," [20] I see the fundamental connection finally clarified only in the reality of God and therefore the revelation of God. Much nineteenth- and twentieth-century theology has aborted by beginning theological analogies from

human experience and trying to proceed from there to the
experience of God. Under the analogical procedure which
I have previously outlined,[21] the most illuminating analogy
proceeds from the self-disclosure of God to human self-
disclosure, from divine empathy, congruence, and acceptance to human empathy, congruence, and acceptance.
Such an analogy can proceed meaningfully and modestly
without becoming embroiled in the fruitless jurisdictional
dispute between theology and therapy with which Williams' book tends to become preoccupied.

b. *The principle of "linkage,"* which is the methodological center of Williams' proposed analogy, is based
upon a social process conception of reality which argues
that "Man, God's creature, is the being who finds every
part of his experience linked with every other part . . .
actually or potentially." [22] Upon this basis he consistently
reads the analogy symbolically from the manward side to
the being of God, so that: "A struggle to understand another person becomes a symbol of the mind's search for
understanding life itself or God himself. Loving devotion
to a sick person becomes a sacrament of the spirit of God
who cares for all. . . . The hunger of the body may become the symbolic expression of the hunger of the soul for
God." [23] However true it may be that "once we have
grasped the principle of linkage we see how meaningless
a sharp distinction between therapy and salvation becomes," [24] the more crucial issue is the definition of the
link itself. For Bonhoeffer, the link is Christ, God's own
worldly involvement.[25] For Williams, the link is a natural
fact with no final dependence upon the unique self-disclosure of God in history. Thus in the last analysis Williams'
analogy between therapy and salvation proceeds on the
basis of a natural theology which proposes to derive knowledge of God from the organismic character of human experience, a procedure for which we have already stated our
reasons for rejecting. Although the treatment of analogy
by Don Browning stands in much the same tradition and
manifests many of the same virtues and limitations as

Williams', it is unique in that it attempts to employ the
analogia fidei within the context of process philosophy.[26]
It is also worth noting that the same principle of "linkage" was anticipated by David Roberts, who earlier wrote:
"Theology has always sought to express doctrinally this
linkage between Christ and the universally human." [27] The
"link" of which they speak, however, was spoken of in an
earlier period as a "point of contact" between man and
God upon which one could base a theological interpretation of the natural. If most of the theological voices in dialogue with therapy have taken Brunner's side of that no-
torious argument, we wish to explore (with Bonhoeffer as
our major companion) the implications the stubborn No
of Barth and Barmen for this dialogue.[28]

5. The Claim of Psychotherapy Upon Theological Imagination

Our argument for the cosmic scope of the Christ event
leaves two questions: How is this universalism consistent
with the claim of the kerygma that the love of God is only
knowable as fully self-revealed in a special history of the
people of Israel and of the Christ? And, Upon what basis
does psychotherapy make its special claim upon theological reflection, i.e., How is the particularity and uniqueness
of Christ's formation in the therapeutic process related to
our broader assertion of the cosmic scope of the Christ
event? If these questions have lain dormant ever since our
initial study of Bonhoeffer and Teilhard, they must now,
however briefly, be brought to light and examined with
clarity.

An adequate clarification might profitably plunge us
into a complex theological issue with many nuances and a
long history, viz., the question of how the action of God in
universal history is related to the unique deed of God in a
special history which illuminates the meaning of God's
action in the whole of history. We must be content, without diverting our argument on therapy into an introverted
theological monologue, with making these two minimal

assertions: (*a*) The God of the Biblical witness is a living participant in the totality of universal history. Negatively this means the rejection of the view that God is active at some points of *kairos* and not at others, or that the presence of God in salvation history implies an absence of God in universal history. (*b*) The God of the Biblical witness encounters and deals with the whole of history and the cosmos proleptically and prototypically through a special history, the history of the people of Israel and the Christ, so as to illuminate his purposes and presence in and for the whole. Negatively we reject the view that the presence of God in universal history renders meaningless or useless the special action of God in the history of Israel. Thus to bifurcate *Heilsgeschichte* and universal history as distinct theological alternatives is to misunderstand the Biblical witness to the God who acts in the one for the many.[29]

But in what sense does psychotherapy deserve to be treated by theology as a special case, a very particular process which may be seen uniquely to be illuminated under the analogy of divine love? At least it is clear, wholly apart from any theological talk, that effective psychotherapy differs markedly from most ordinary human relationships and conversations, involving greater intimacy, more intensive self-disclosure, and a deeper penetration of the realities of guilt and forgiveness than most common human encounters. Our discussion has implied, however, that effective psychotherapy is a *unique* process of self-disclosure and a special crystallization of empathetic understanding and unconditional positive regard, and that (more than other natural and historical processes) it often may actually mediate, concretize, and embody the divine forgiving love which is finally clarified once for all in Jesus Christ.

It must be clear by now that in our view it is not the therapeutic process which clarifies the love of God, but the love of God which finally clarifies the internal reality of the therapeutic process. But it remains to be shown why psychotherapy is sufficiently unique so as to be singled out among other human processes for this analogical attention. How is therapeutic dialogue essentially different from an economic transaction, or education or parental love, or from the drop of a coin in the natural-physical order, so as to plunge it into this special orbit of theological interpretation? What constitutes its uniqueness as a mirror of God's self-disclosure?

The answer: Psychotherapy and it alone has made a deliberate science and a medical art out of the study of the process of mediating the very empathetic understanding and unconditional positive regard which from another perspective is the ultimate concern of theology. The therapeutic process itself is not the unique property or preserve of psychotherapy, since it belongs to human experience generally, and can be seen to operate in all sorts of relationships besides professional psychotherapy. But to make of these processes a deliberate object of empirical inquiry and to nurture them into a professional tradition of medical praxis is something quite different, and constitutes the unique claim of psychotherapy upon theological imagination and attention.

Over against therapists who stress diagnostic techniques, our discussion finds its natural ally more in those therapists from Rank to Rogers who have de-emphasized objectifying diagnosis in favor of a stress upon the quality and depth of the interpersonal relationship as the real focus of therapeutic help. Admittedly the crucial therapeutic forces of empathy, congruence, and unconditional acceptance may appear powerfully in the nonprofessional relationships of father and son, husband and wife, student and teacher, etc. Although not limited to professional therapy, these dynamics have been studied, clarified, and refined into a medical art by professional therapists and clinical psychologists, but the dynamics themselves may be found potentially wherever human beings meet.

This leads us finally to propose this hypothesis for discussion: *The " therapeutic relationship " is nothing other than a relation of authenticity with another*. We do not mean to imply that the healing arts must now try to convert all human relationships into something supposedly "therapeutic," thus transforming human society into a hospital. In fact, we mean virtually the opposite, that the hospital needs to be converted into an authentic world. The locus of healing is authentic human community. What is being described by clinicians as health-producing (openness, congruence, acceptance, empathy, etc.) actually belongs to the definition of any authentic human relationship, and not "psychotherapy" only. Actual therapeutic dynamics have thus been the interest of theology long before modern psychotherapy appeared on the scene, although they remained inadequately clarified as such. If so, then the health-producing elements in professional psychotherapy and psychiatric care are not at all their professional aspects (although these are necessary) but essentially their *human* aspects, the rich dynamics of human authenticity, in relation to which the process of professionalization must always remain the servant.

Epilogue

" Worldly talk of God is concrete talk of God. We know from numerous disappointments and our own manifold failures that talk of God mostly persists in non-committal and ineffective generalities. For that reason it provokes no opposition, yet neither is it heeded in revolutionizing ways, but spreads abroad that possibly tranquillizing, but actually killing, atmosphere of unimportance and boredom which is the death of faith. Already most people expect nothing else from talk of God." [1]

If our own speech about God is to avoid the tranquilliz-ing irrelevance of which Ebeling here speaks, it must di-rect itself simply toward the here and now world in which God is making himself known concretely. But to know the world concretely as God knows it in Jesus Christ, instead of abstractly as it knows itself apart from God, is to know it as always already loved, judged, and understood by its source and ground.

What we are calling worldly theology is actually merely an ecumenical (Chalcedonian) Christology in dialogue with the secular mind. Such thinking rejects, on the one hand, all allegedly high Christologies which ignore or withdraw from the world, failing to witness to the pres-ence of Christ in the midst of the world, and on the other hand, all allegedly realistic cosmologies which fail to take seriously the seriousness with which God himself has taken the world. The uniqueness of worldly theology (in contrast to untheological views of the world and unworldly views of theology) is its equal insistence both upon the high Christology and upon the worldly character of the love of God, understood not as two different commitments but as a single one, single-mindedly dealing with the Christ who always shares in the life of the world and the world which already shares in the life of the Christ.

This is the style of theologizing which we propose to apply to the dialogue with psychotherapy, conversing with therapy not merely on its own limited basis but upon the basis of its already being known, understood, and under-girded by God in Jesus Christ. Such a dialogue does not allow its partner the crippling illusion that his assumptions are fully adequate and complete in ignorance of God's oc-curring love, but instead begins at a wholly confessional beginning point, listening to the internal reality of the partner in dialogue at a level of depth which he himself may not hear. Dialogue in worldly theology thus means not merely exchanging views or listening to the world so as to take seriously its illusions about itself, but an at-tempt at listening to the neighbor at a depth deeper than he himself is able to hear, namely, the level of depth at which God himself hears and understands, and speaking to the neighbor unapologetically of the speech of God which is already present in his existence even when we fail to point to it adequately with our own human speech.

Notes

Abbreviations

AB	Act and Being
CB	The Courage to Be
CD	Church Dogmatics
FJC	The Finality of Jesus Christ in the Age of Universal History
HU	Hymn of the Universe
K&C	Kerygma and Counseling
KM	Kerygma and Myth
MD	Le Milieu Divin
NRS	No Rusty Swords
OBP	On Becoming a Person
PC	Pastoral Counseling
PFG	Prisoner for God
PPT	Preface to Pastoral Theology
PrC	Primitive Christianity
SC	Sanctorum Communio
ST	Systematic Theology
TC	Theology of Culture
TNT	Theology of the New Testament
TPC	A Theology of Pastoral Care

Notes

Introduction

1. Notably Tillich, Roberts, and Outler; cf. Chapters V and IX for critical comments. See also Victor White, *God and the Unconscious* (London: The Harvill Press, Ltd., 1952), and Lewis J. Sherrill, *Guilt and Redemption* (John Knox Press, 1945; revised, 1957).

2. We will not elaborate a detailed bibliography of these efforts, but for a critical review of many of them, see Thomas C. Oden, "Revelation in Psychotherapy," in *Continuum*, Summer, 1964. The sheer quantity of this literature would lead one to suspect that something exciting must be happening in this area. Indeed, some of these contributions are in some respects quite good; cf. especially Hans Schär, *Seelsorge und Psychotherapie* (Zurich: Rascher, 1961); Wayne E. Oates, *Protestant Pastoral Counseling* (The Westminster Press, 1962); W. Kurth and G. Bartning, *Psychotherapie in der Seelsorge* (Munich: Ernst Reinhardt, 1964); Dayton G. Van Deusen, *Redemptive Counseling* (John Knox Press, 1960); Edward E. Thornton, *Theology and Pastoral Counseling* (Prentice-Hall, Inc., 1964); Helmut Harsch, *Das Schuldproblem in Theologie und Tiefenpsychologie* (Heidelberg: Quelle und Meyer, 1965); as well as some of the essays in the *Arzt und Seelsorger* series ed. by Wilhelm Bitter (Ernst Klett Verlag, 1955 ff.). A closer inspection of this literature as a whole, however, will reveal that it has not enlisted the best efforts of the current generation of theologians, and especially that competent Biblical and systematic theologians have not shared very meaningfully in the framing of its questions. For additional bibliography, one may consult Van Deusen, *op. cit.*, pp. 179 ff.; Thornton, *op. cit.*, pp. 137 ff.

3. Norman O. Brown, *Life Against Death* (Random House, Inc., 1959); Erik Erikson, *Insight and Responsibility* (W. W. Norton & Company, Inc., 1964); O. Hobart Mowrer, *The Crisis in Psychiatry and Religion* (D. Van Nostrand Company, Inc., 1961); Abraham H. Maslow, *Toward a Psychology of Being* (D. Van Nostrand Company, Inc., 1962).

4. Friedrich Gogarten, *Der Mensch zwischen Gott und*

Welt (Stuttgart: Friedrich Vorwork-Verlag, 1956); Rudolf
Bultmann, *History and Eschatology* (Edinburgh: Edinburgh
University Press, 1955); Dietrich Bonhoeffer, *Prisoner for God,*
ed. by Eberhard Bethge; tr. by Reginald Fuller (The Macmil-
lan Company, 1954); James M. Robinson, Martin Noth, *et al.,*
"The Problem of a New Testament Theology," *The Bultmann
School of Biblical Interpretations: New Directions,* ed. by
Robert W. Funk (Harper & Row, Publishers, Inc., 1965);
Gabriel Vahanian, *The Death of God* (George Braziller, Inc.,
1961).

    5. *Offenbarung als Geschichte,* ed. by Wolfhart Pannenberg
(Göttingen: Vandenhoeck & Ruprecht, 1963); Yves Congar,
O. P., *Lay People in the Church* (The Newman Press, 1965);
Schubert M. Ogden, "Bultmann's Demythologizing and Hart-
shorne's Dipolar Theism," *Process and Divinity — The Hart-
shorne Festschrift,* ed. by William L. Reese and Eugene Free-
man (The Open Court Publishing Co., 1962); Jürgen Moltmann, *Theologie der Hoffnung* (Munich: Chr. Kaiser Verlag,
1965).

    6. Adolf Köberle, "Das Schuldproblem in theologischer
und tiefenpsychologischer Sicht," *Psychotherapie und Seelsorge,* ed. by Wilhelm Bitter (Ernst Klett Verlag, 1960). In Europe a far greater contribution to this dialogue has been made
by physicians than by theologians. Cf. Viktor von Weizsäcker,
Menschenführung (Göttingen: Vandenhoeck & Ruprecht,
1955); Theodor Bovet, *Lebendige Seelsorge* (Tübingen: Katz-
man, 1954); Victor Emil von Gebsattel, *Imago Hominis*
(Schweinfurt: Verlag Neues Forum, 1964); Paul Tournier, *The
Meaning of Persons* (London: SCM Press, Ltd., 1957); Karl
Stern, *The Third Revolution* (Image Books, 1961); W. Küte-
meyer, *Die Krankheit in ihrer Menschlichkeit* (Göttingen:
Vandenhoeck & Ruprecht, 1963).

    7. Daniel Day Williams, *The Minister and the Care of Souls*
(Harper & Brothers, 1961). In fact, one of the most telling aspects of the world Consultation of Psychiatrists and Theologians in Switzerland in 1966 was the noticeable absence of any
leading systematic theologians from either the U.S. or Europe,
with the exception of Köberle. To be sure, other recent contributions have come from the side of pastoral psychology and
counseling. Cf. especially Oates and Thornton, *op. cit.,* as well
as William E. Hulme, *Counseling and Theology* (Muhlenberg
Press, 1956); Charles Stinnette, *Faith, Freedom and Selfhood*
(The Seabury Press, Inc., 1959); Frederic Greeves, *Theology
and the Cure of Souls: An Introduction to Pastoral Theology*
(London: The Epworth Press, Publishers, 1960); Peder Olsen,
Pastoral Care and Psychotherapy (Augsburg Publishing House,
1961); and E. N. Ducker, *Psychotherapy: A Christian Approach* (London: George Allen & Unwin, Ltd., 1964); but the
absence of significant and sustained contribution from system-

atic theologians and exegetes is indeed regrettable. The promising efforts of Aarne Siirala, *The Voice of Illness* (Fortress Press, 1964), and Don S. Browning, *Psychotherapy and Atonement* (The Westminster Press, 1966), are perhaps exceptions to this trend, for they much more adequately manage to bring a well-equipped and consistent theological perspective to bear upon the operational questions in pastoral care.

8. T. S. Szasz, " The Myth of Mental Illness," *American Psychologist*, Vol. XV (1960), pp. 113–118; H. J. Eysenck, " The Effects of Psychotherapy: An Evaluation," *Journal Consult. Psychol.*, Vol. XVI (1952), pp. 319–324; Mowrer, *op. cit.*; Maslow, *op. cit.*

9. To be more explicit, it is precisely a special theme of ethics — the question of the good life (authenticity, full-functioning, maturity, health, human completeness) — which has led the author down this circuitous path into the study of psychotherapy, which forcefully sets before man a certain understanding of human self-fulfillment, what human existence ought to be, values worth striving for — in short, the question of the good. So we regard it as hopelessly artificial to try to make a strict separation of fields of ethics, psychology, and theology.

CHAPTER I.   A Theology of the Saeculum

1. *Die mündige Welt* (Munich: Chr. Kaiser Verlag, 1955 ff.), Vols. I–IV.

2. Likewise in the briefer American assessment of *The Place of Bonhoeffer,* ed. by Martin E. Marty (Association Press, 1956), it is also telling that no reference is made to Bonhoeffer's significance for psychotherapy. Only Thornton, *op. cit.*, pp. 39 ff., and Sürala, *op. cit.*, pp. 139 ff., have begun to develop this theme.

3. For autobiographical reference, see John D. Godsey, *The Theology of Dietrich Bonhoeffer* (The Westminster Press, 1960).

4. Dietrich Bonhoeffer, *Ethics,* ed. by Eberhard Bethge; tr. by Neville Horton Smith (London: SCM Press, Ltd., 1955), pp. 62 ff.

5. Gordon W. Allport, *The Individual and His Religion* (The Macmillan Company, 1950), *passim;* Hans Asmussen, *Die Seelsorge* (Munich: Chr. Kaiser Verlag, 1934); Eduard Thurneysen, *A Theology of Pastoral Care,* tr. by Jack Worthington, Thomas Weiser, *et al.* (John Knox Press, 1962), pp. 54–68; Tournier, *op. cit.*, pp. 102–123; Josef Goldbrunner, *Cure of Mind and Cure of Soul* (University of Notre Dame Press, 1963), pp. 23 ff.; Fulton Sheen, *Peace of Soul* (Whittlesey House, 1949), *passim.*

6. *Ethics,* p. 63.

7. *Ethics,* p. 63.

8. Sigmund Freud, *Moses and Monotheism* (Alfred A.

Knopf, Inc., 1949); Erich Fromm, *Psychoanalysis and Religion* (Yale University Press, 1950).

9. Wilhelm Löhe, *Gesammelte Werke* (Neuendettelsau: Freimund-Verlag, 1951 ff.), Vols. I–VII; Göte Bergsten, *Pastoral Psychology, A Study in the Care of Souls* (The Macmillan Company, 1951); Olsen, *op. cit.*

10. Allport, *op. cit.;* C. J. Jung, *Psychology and Religion* (Yale University Press, 1938); Mowrer, *op. cit.*

11. Stern, *op. cit.;* Russell L. Dicks, *Toward Health and Wholeness* (The Macmillan Company, 1960); Paul E. Johnson, *Psychology of Pastoral Care* (Abingdon Press, 1953).

12. *Ethics*, pp. 63–64.

13. *Ethics*, pp. 61, 62.

14. *Ethics*, p. 64.

15. *Ethics*, p. 68. Cf. Gerhard Ebeling, *Word and Faith* (London: SCM Press, Ltd., 1963), pp. 283–284n.

16. *Ethics*, p. 8.

17. *Ethics*, pp. 65, 66.

18. Carl P. Rogers, *On Becoming a Person* (Houghton Mifflin Company, 1961), pp. 31–59. Cf. Thomas C. Oden, *Kerygma and Counseling* (The Westminster Press, 1966), Ch. I.

19. Rudolf Bultmann, *Jesus Christ and Mythology* (Charles Scribner's Sons, 1958). This distinction is defended by this writer in *Radical Obedience* (The Westminster Press, 1964), Ch. II, and "The Alleged Structural Inconsistency in Bultmann," *The Journal of Religion*, July, 1964, pp. 194 ff.

20. *PFG*, p. 172.

21. Dietrich Bonhoeffer, *Act and Being*, tr. by Bernard Noble (Harper & Brothers, 1962), p. 183.

22. *AB*, p. 181; cf. pp. 13, 28, 180–184; Dietrich Bonhoeffer, *Sanctorum Communio*, tr. by R. Gregor Smith (London: William Collins Sons & Co., Ltd., 1963), pp. 166–167; Dietrich Bonhoeffer, *No Rusty Swords*, ed. by Edwin H. Robertson and John Bowden (Harper & Row, Publishers, Inc., 1965), pp. 65, 372.

23. *Ethics*, p. 293.

24. *NRS*, pp. 108–109.

25. *Ethics*, p. 294. Bonhoeffer is quick to avoid a serious misunderstanding on this point, however: "The emancipation of the worldly order under the dominion of Christ takes concrete form not through the conversion of Christian statesmen, etc., but through the concrete encounter of the secular institutions with the Church of Jesus Christ, her proclamation, her life." Psychotherapy will not be truly free for worldly functioning until it sees its own process reflected in the light of the kerygma. Its fuller emancipation awaits a concrete encounter with authentic Christian community with its explicit word celebrated in preaching and sacrament.

26. *Ethics*, p. 296.

27. *Ethics*, p. 103. Bonhoeffer employs a sharp distinction between *creatura* and *natura:* " Through the fall the ' creature ' becomes ' nature,' " p. 102.

28. *Ethics*, p. 102.

29. Karen Horney, *Neurosis and Human Growth* (W. W. Norton & Company, Inc., 1950); Kurt Goldstein, *Human Nature from the Point of View of Psychopathology* (Harvard University Press, 1940); Rogers, *OBP*, p. 351; Maslow, *op. cit.*

30. *Ethics*, p. 105.

31. Carl P. Rogers, *Client-centered Therapy* (Houghton Mifflin Company, 1951), Part I.

32. *Ethics*, p. 106.

33. *Ethics*, p. 105.

34. Dietrich Bonhoeffer, *The Cost of Discipleship*, tr. by R. H. Fuller (The Macmillan Company, 1958), p. 195. Cf. *Ethics*, pp. 17–25.

35. *Ethics*, pp. 18, 19. Formation is not a question of applying to the world the " teaching of Christ, or what are referred to as Christian principles, so that the world might be formed in accordance with these," nor is it " an ideal to be striven after," but simply " being drawn into the form of Jesus Christ " (*Ethics*, p. 18 and *Cost of Discipleship*, p. 195). So crucial is this construct for Bonhoeffer's ethics that he remarks, " Indeed it is wrong to speak of the Christian life; we should speak rather of Christ living in us " (*Cost of Discipleship*, p. 197).

36. *Ethics*, pp. 20–21.

37. With Bonhoeffer, we flatly disavow any vague, generalized notion of an " invisible " church. Cf. *SC*, pp. 144 ff. His rejection of " religion " can in no sense be cynically read as a rejection of the church in the most objective, historical, and empirical sense.

38. John 1:11; Col. 1:17.

39. *Ethics*, p. 293.

40. *Ethics*, p. 325.

41. *Ethics*, pp. 70–71.

Chapter II.   Bonhoeffer's Theology and Religionless Psychotherapy

1. *PFG*, pp. 121–123.

2. *PFG*, p. 157.

3. *PFG*, pp. 142–143.

4. *PFG*, pp. 145–146.

5. *PFG*, p. 146.

6. *PFG*, p. 163. Note, however, that it is only " before God " that we can truly live *etsi deus non daretur.* " We have to live in the world *etsi deus non daretur*. And this is just what we do — before God! " (P. 163.)

7. *PFG*, p. 163.

8. *PFG*, pp. 140–141.

9. Karl Barth, *Church Dogmatics* (Edinburgh: T. & T. Clark, 1936 ff.), Vol. I/2, pp. 280–362 (sec. 17).

10. *PFG*, p. 123.

11. *PFG*, pp. 124, 156, 164.

12. Jung, Fromm, and Allport, *op. cit.*; Henry Guntrip, *Psychotherapy and Religion* (Harper & Brothers, 1957); W. Earl Biddle, *Integration of Religion and Psychiatry* (Collier Books, 1962); John G. McKenzie, *Nervous Disorders and Religion* (Collier Books, 1962).

13. *PFG*, p. 146 (letter of June 8, 1944).

14. *PFG*, p. 159 (letter of July 8, 1944).

15. *PFG*, p. 158.

16. *PFG*, pp. 158–159.

17. *PFG*, p. 160.

18. *SC*, p. 35.

19. *OBP*, pp. 152–153.

20. *OBP*, p. 188.

21. *Ethics*, p. 197.

22. *Ethics*, p. 10.

23. *Ethics*, p. 12: " The despiser of men despises what God has loved." It is so easy to despise that which is caught in inauthenticity, guilt, and anxiety, both in ourselves and others. The therapist meets such bondage with unconditional positive regard. Yet for Bonhoeffer, it is only in the light of the incarnation, in which we see ourselves as having been loved by God as real men, that it becomes possible in a fuller sense to accept the real man before us, to achieve empathetic acceptance. " It is only through God's being made man that it is possible to know the real man and not to despise him. The real man can live before God, and we can allow the real man to live before God side by side with ourselves without either despising or deifying him." (P. 12.)

24. *Ethics*, p. 84.

25. *Ethics*, p. 85.

26. *Ethics*, p. 85. Cf. Edward E. Thornton, *op. cit.*, p. 39.

27. *PFG*, p. 164.

28. *PFG*, p. 164.

29. Rogers, "Client-centered Therapy: A Current View," *Progress in Psychotherapy*, ed. by Frieda Fromm-Reichmann and J. L. Moreno (Grune & Stratton, Inc., 1956), pp. 199–209.

30. *PFG*, p. 147.

31. *PFG*, pp. 147–148.

32. *PFG*, p. 124.

33. *Ethics*, p. 320.

34. *Ethics*, p. 320. Cf. *CD*, II/1.

35. *PFG*, pp. 148 f.

36. *PFG*, p. 123. Cf. Godsey, *op. cit.*, pp. 276 ff. Also *AB*, pp. 101 ff.

37. *PFG*, p. 125.
38. *NRS*, pp. 361–372.
39. Cf. Pannenberg, Moltmann, *op. cit.*

CHAPTER III. The Divine Milieu

1. Pierre Teilhard de Chardin, *Le Milieu Divin*, tr. by Bernard Wall, *et al.* (London: William Collins Sons & Co., Ltd., 1960), p. 76. The dedication page reads: "For those who love the world."

2. Pierre Teilhard de Chardin, *Letters from a Traveller*, ed. by Claude Aragonnès; tr. by René Hague, *et al.* (London: William Collins Sons & Co., Ltd., 1962).

3. Henri de Lubac, *The Faith of Teilhard de Chardin* (London: Burns, Oates, & Washbourne, Ltd., 1964).

4. Julian Huxley, Introduction to *Letters from a Traveller*, pp. 13 ff.

5. *MD*, p. 70.
6. *MD*, p. 130n.
7. *MD*, p. 67.
8. *MD*, p. 112.

9. Pierre Teilhard de Chardin, *Hymn of the Universe* (Harper & Row, Publishers, Inc., 1961), p. 84.

10. *HU*, p. 84.
11. *HU*, p. 87.
12. *HU*, p. 89.
13. *HU*, p. 80, quoted from "Le Milieu Mystique" (1917).
14. *HU*, p. 89.
15. *HU*, pp. 13–14.
16. *HU*, pp. 19–20.
17. *HU*, p. 23.
18. *HU*, p. 20.
19. *HU*, pp. 36 f.
20. *HU*, p. 79.
21. *MD*, pp. 65, 68.
22. *MD*, p. 123.
23. *MD*, p. 114.
24. *MD*, p. 66.
25. *MD*, p. 116; cf. p. 130.
26. *MD*, p. 53.
27. *MD*, p. 122. Cf. Bonhoeffer, *Ethics*, pp. 61, 301: "In him all things hold together" (Col. 1:17). It should be clear that Teilhard and Bonhoeffer are merely giving new expression to a basic cosmological viewpoint that has been vigorously present and available in the Christian tradition from the first century, which holds that the Christ event epiphanies the inner meaning of the cosmos. This theme, powerfully expressed in the view of Irenaeus that the whole history of man and creation is recapitulated in the incarnation, can also be found in Augustine, the

medieval mystics, Calvin, Coccejus, and much of the Reformed tradition from Beza to Barth which views creation under the image of covenant.

CHAPTER IV.   Tillich's Theology of Culture

1. " The Theology of Pastoral Care," *Christian Advocate,* June 23, 1960; " Theology and Counseling," *Journal of Pastoral Care,* Winter, 1956; " On Healing," *Pastoral Psychology,* June, 1955; "Karen Horney" (a funeral address), *Pastoral Psychology,* May, 1953; " The Person in Technical Society," *Christian Faith and Social Action,* ed. by John A. Hutchison (Charles Scribner's Sons, 1953), pp. 137–153; " Human Nature Can Change," *American Journal of Psychoanalysis,* Vol. XII, No. 1 (1952), pp. 65–67; " The Impact of Pastoral Psychology on Theological Thought," *The Ministry and Mental Health,* ed. by H. Hofmann (Association Press, 1960), Ch. 1; " The Relevance of the Ministry in Our Time and Its Theological Foundation," *Making the Ministry Relevant,* ed. by Hans Hofmann (Charles Scribner's Sons, 1960); "Psychotherapy and a Christian Interpretation of Human Nature," *Review of Religion,* March, 1949; " The Relation of Religion and Health," *Pastoral Psychology,* May, 1954, reprinted in *Healing: Human and Divine,* ed. by S. Doniger (Association Press, 1957); " Religion and Secular Culture," *Journal of Religion,* April, 1946; " The Lost Dimension of Religion," *Saturday Evening Post,* June 14, 1958; " You Are Accepted," *Shaking of the Foundations* (Charles Scribner's Sons, 1948), Ch. 19; " Communicating the Gospel," *Pastoral Psychology,* June, 1956.

2. Paul Tillich, " Psychoanalysis, Existentialism and Theology," *Pastoral Psychology,* Oct., 1958; appeared in revised form in *Theology of Culture,* ed. by Robert C. Kimball (Oxford University Press, Inc., 1959), pp. 112–127.

3. *TC,* p. 124.

4. Johannes Hamel, " The Proclamation of the Gospel in the Marxist World," Karl Barth and Johannes Hamel, *How to Serve God in a Marxist Land* (Association Press, 1959), pp. 84–126. Cf. Oden, " The Gospel Knows No Iron Curtain," *Christian Advocate,* June, 1959.

5. Paul Tillich, *Systematic Theology* (London: James Nisbet & Co., Ltd., 1953), Vol. I, pp. 3–14; (The University of Chicago Press. 1957), Vol. II, pp. 13 ff.

6. *ST,* II, p. 13.

7. *ST,* II, p. 9.

8. Tillich specifically repudiates the proper name " Jesus Christ " as a theological construct, in favor of " Jesus who is called the Christ " or " Jesus as the Christ," *ST, II,* pp. 97–98.

9. *ST,* II, p. 94. Patristic Christology, of course, also rejected the view that God ceases to be God, for it is precisely amid his full participation in human existence that God shows

himself most radically to be God.

10. *ST*, II, p. 95.
11. *ST*, II, p. 95.
12. *ST*, II, p. 99.
13. *ST*, II, p. 99.
14. *ST*, II, p. 150. Cf. Karl Barth, *Rudolf Bultmann: Ein Versuch, ihn zu verstehen* (Zollikon-Zurich: Evangelischer Verlag, 1953).
15. Paul Tillich, *The Courage to Be* (Yale University Press, 1952), p. 165.
16. *CB*, p. 166.
17. *ST*, II, p. 107.
18. *CB*, p. 176.
19. *CB*, p. 177 (italics mine).
20. *CB*, p. 77 (cf. Ch. 3, *passim*). Tillich feared the possibility of pastors engaging in what he called "amateur psychotherapeutic activities." "The relevance of the Christian ministry will be decreased if, along with their functions as club directors, pressure group agents and educators, many of our younger ministers also consider themselves as dilettante psychoanalysts. There is no doubt that this is a danger today" (*Making the Ministry Relevant,* ed. by Hans Hofmann), p. 25. We fully agree, if by psychoanalysis Tillich is referring to the Freudian model, as we suspect he is, that requires very special skills in diagnosis, dream interpretation, and transference. But in the broader sense in which Rogers speaks of "the helping relationship" of empathy, congruence, and positive regard, all this is directly germane to the church's ministry, and the pastor would do well to embody just such therapeutic attitudes in his parish relationships. (Cf. "The Theology of Pastoral Care," *loc. cit.*)
21. *TC*, pp. 122–123.
22. Ludwig Binswanger, *Ausgewählte Vorträge und Aufsätze* (Bern: Francke, 1955); V. E. von Gebsattel, *op. cit.*; V. von Weizsäcker, *op. cit.*; V. Frankl, *Man's Search for Meaning* (Washington Square Press, Inc., 1963); J. H. van den Berg, *The Changing Nature of Man* (Dell Publishing Company, Inc., 1964); Medard Boss, *Psychoanalysis and Daseinsanalysis* (Basic Books, Inc., Publishers, 1963).
23. Tillich, "The Theology of Pastoral Care," *loc. cit.*, p. 4.
24. Paul Tillich, *The New Being* (Charles Scribner's Sons, 1955), p. 39.
25. *ST*, III, p. 280.
26. *CD*, IV/2, pp. 511–533.
27. *TC*, pp. 112 ff. Cf. Horney, *op. cit.*
28. *ST*, II, p. 44. Cf. Oden, *Radical Obedience*, p. 20.
29. Tillich, "The Theology of Pastoral Care," *loc. cit.*, p. 4.
30. *ST*, II, p. 135.
31. *Journal of Pastoral Care*, Winter, 1956. Cf. "The Theol-

ogy of Pastoral Care," *loc. cit.*, p. 5. Cf. " Theology and Counseling," *loc. cit.*

32. Although Tillich criticizes natural theology on the
grounds that it attempts to make affirmations about God on the
basis of man's finitude (*ST*, I, p. 133), elsewhere he argues that
" the *analogia entis* gives us our only justification of speaking
at all about God. It is based on the fact that God must be understood as being-itself" (*ST*, I, p. 240). "Without such an
analogy nothing could be said about God." (*ST*, I, p. 131.)
Tillich wishes to read the analogy in both Godward and manward directions, a procedure we have elsewhere criticized
(*K & C*, Chs. II and IV. Cf. *ST*, I, p. 267; II, p. 115).

CHAPTER V.   Thurneysen's Kerygmatic *Seelsorge*

1. *TPC*, p. 54.
2. *TPC*, p. 53; cf. p. 108.
3. *TPC*, p. 84.
4. *TPC*, p. 92. Cf. Thurneysen, *Seelsorge und Psychotherapie* (Munich: Chr. Kaiser Verlag, 1950), *passim.*
5. *TPC*, p. 226.
6. *TPC*, p. 83.
7. *TPC*, p. 245. Cf. *Gottesdienst und Menschendienst* (Zol-
likon: Evangelischer Verlag, 1958).
8. *TPC*, p. 213.
9. Mowrer, *op. cit.*, pp. 40 ff.
10. *TPC*, p. 208. Cf. von Gebsattel, Boss, *op. cit.;* Igor A.
Caruso, *Existential Psychology* (Herder & Herder, Inc., 1964);
Maslow, Rogers, *op. cit; The Self,* ed. by Moustakas (Harper &
Brothers, 1956); *Existence,* ed. by Rollo May (Basic Books,
Inc., Publishers, 1958).
11. *TPC*, pp. 200–201. Cf. *Christ und Welt* (Basel, 1950).
12. *TPC*, p 245.
13. *TPC*, p. 246; cf. pp. 247–249.
14. II Cor. 10:5.
15. *TPC*, p. 108 (italics mine).
16. *TPC*, p. 109. " The content of pastoral care is identical
with that of public preaching, but here it assumes a private
form" (p. 15). Cf. Thornton, *op. cit.*, pp. 48 ff.
17. *TPC*, p. 15. Cf. Asmussen, *op. cit*, pp. 15 ff.
18. *TPC*, p. 109.
19. *TPC*, p. 109.
20. *TPC*, p. 52.
21. *K&C*, Ch. II.
22. *TPC*, p. 92.
23. *TPC*, p. 92. Cf. *Seelsorge und Psychotherapie.*
24. *TPC*, p. 106.
25. CD, Vol. III, *op. cit., passim.*
26. *TPC*, p. 106; Acts 17:28.
27. *TPC*, p. 78.

CHAPTER VI.   Hiltner's Operation-centered Pastoral Theology

1. Seward Hiltner, *The Counselor in Counseling* (Abingdon Press, 1950), p. 11.

2. Seward Hiltner, *Pastoral Counseling* (Abingdon Press, 1949), p. 19.

3. *PC*, p. 34.

4. *PC*, p. 34. Cf. Seward Hiltner, *Preface to Pastoral Theology* (Abingdon Press, 1958), pp. 20 ff.

5. *PC*, p. 122 (italics mine).

6. W. A. Visser 't Hooft, "Pluralism — Temptation or Opportunity," *Ecumenical Review*, April, 1966, pp. 129 ff.

7. *CD*, II/1, *passim*.

8. *PC*, p. 153.

9. *PC*, p. 155.

10. *PC*, pp. 125–148.

11. *PC*, p. 153.

12. *PC*, p. 155; cf. p. 156.

13. *PC*, pp. 155 ff. Cf. *PPT*, pp. 177 ff.

14. *PC*, pp. 187–226.

15. *PFG*, *passim*. Cf. Carroll A. Wise, *Pastoral Counseling, Its Theory and Practice* (Harper & Brothers, 1951), pp. 144 ff.

16. *PC*, p. 194.

17. *PC*, p. 193.

18. *PC*, 202–209 (italics mine).

19. *PC*, p. 202.

20. *PC*, p. 217.

21. *PPT*, p. 182.

22. *PPT*, p. 218.

23. *PPT*, p. 20.

24. *PC*, p. 253.

25. *PC*, pp. 253 ff.

26. *PPT*, p. 29.

27. *PPT*, p. 18.

28. John Deschner, editorial introduction to *The Student World*, First Quarter, 1954, pp. 1 ff.

CHAPTER VII.   Exegetical Considerations

1. The special understanding of exegesis which we are here employing is that spelled out by Bonhoeffer in his 1935 lecture on "The Interpretation of the New Testament" (*NRS*, pp. 308–325), in which he argues that the intention of exegesis "should not be to justify Christianity in this present age, but *to justify the present age before the Christian message*. Interpretation then means that the present age is brought before the forum of the Christian message" and not otherwise (p. 310). In this lecture he brilliantly clarified what he meant by the "making present" of Biblical texts: "For presentation means that Christ himself speaks . . . that Christ comes to *present*

himself to us, not that we find a general truth confirmed in the New Testament" (p. 320). He contrasts this understanding of exegesis with all other types of interpretation that proceed by trying to discover something of eternal validity or some ethical norm in the text, or in other words, any interpretation in which "the truth is already established before I begin to expound Scripture" (p. 313). If some readers may be disappointed in our style of exegesis, with only spare references to certain historical-critical questions, we can only point to this lecture as our hermeneutical beginning point for a different understanding of the exegesis itself.

2. *NRS*, p. 316.

3. Col. 1:15, 16. Cf. C. F. D. Moule, *The Epistles of Paul the Apostle to the Colossians and to Philemon* (Cambridge University Press, 1957), p. 61. Also cf. Heb. 1:3, where the Son of God is described as "the heir of all things, through whom also he created the world. He reflects the glory of God and bears the very stamp of his nature, upholding the universe by his word of power."

4. Cf. Rev. 21:6; Eph. 1:19-23.

5. Moffatt: "All coheres in him." Cf. E. F. Scott, *The Epistle of Paul to the Colossians, to Philemon and to the Ephesians* (London: Hodder & Stoughton, Ltd., 1930), p. 21: "In Christ the creation has its source and inner purpose." Cf. Moule, *op. cit.*, p. 67.

6. Cf. "The Lordship of Christ Over the World and the Church" (1959), *Bulletin,* Division of Studies, World Council of Churches, Vol. VIII, No. 2 (Autumn, 1962), pp. 19 ff.

7. *CD*, II/2, pp. 98, 99.

8. *CD*, II/2, sec. 33. Cf. Moule, *op. cit.*, p. 57.

9. Cf. article on "Pas, apas," by Bo Reicke, *Theologisches Wörterbuch zum Neuen Testament,* ed. by Kittel (Stuttgart: Kohlhammer, 1954), pp. 885–895; *A Greek-English Lexicon of the New Testament,* ed. by William F. Arndt and F. Wilbur Gingrich (The University of Chicago Press, 1952), pp. 636, 637.

10. Floyd V. Filson, *A Commentary on the Gospel According to St. Matthew* (London: Adam and Charles Black, Ltd., 1960), p. 267. Cf. Josef Schmid, *Das Evangelium nach Matthäus* (Regensberg: Friedrich Pustet Verlag, 1952), p. 272.

11. *CD*, III/4, "The Unique Opportunity," pp. 565–595.

12. Rudolf Bultmann, *Theology of the New Testament,* Vol. I, pp. 164–165; cf. Chs. 2 and 3.

13. *INT.* Cf. "Gnosis" in *Gerhard Kittel's Bible Key Words,* Vol. II, tr. by J. R. Coates and H. P. Kingdon (London: Adam and Charles Black, Ltd., 1952); Hans Jonas, *The Gnostic Religion* (Beacon Press, Inc., 1958); R. M. Wilson, *The Gnostic Problem* (London: A. R. Mowbray & Company, Ltd., 1958); R. M. Grant, *Gnosticism to Early Christianity* (Columbia University Press, 1959); Dom Jacques Dupont, O.S.B., *Gnosis*

(Paris: Gabalda, 1949). Since our discussion cannot properly be diverted into a detailed analysis of the lengthy and increasing bibliography on gnosticism, these titles must suffice to point to some major contributions to this far-reaching debate. It should be clear, however, that the viewpoint of this inquiry is essentially based on Bultmann's contribution, which in our view has persuasively withstood vigorous attack by its critics.

14. *TNT*, I, p. 165. Cf. Rudolf Bultmann, *Primitive Christianity in Its Contemporary Setting*, tr. by R. H. Fuller (Meridian Books, Inc., 1956), pp. 162 ff.

15. *PrC*, pp. 163 f. Cf. *Gnosis*, pp. 14 ff.; and *TNT*, I, pp. 165–169.

16. Bultmann, *History and Eschatology* (Edinburgh: Edinburgh University Press, 1957), pp. 5, 6; Ch. 1 *passim*. Cf. *PrC*, p. 164.

17. *TNT*, I, pp. 166 f.; *PrC*, p. 163.

18. *PrC*, pp. 154 ff., 163 ff.; *TNT*, I, p. 167.

19. *The New Testament Background: Selected Documents*, ed. by Charles K. Barrett (London: S.P.C.K., 1957), pp. 80–90. Cf. H. Schlier in *Theol. Rundschau* (New Series, 5, 1933), pp. 1–34, 69–92, for a discussion of the relevance of the Mandaean texts as sources for early gnosticism.

20. *TNT*, I, pp. 168 ff.; *PrC*, p. 202.

21. *TNT*, I, pp. 170–183; *PrC*, pp. 200 ff.

22. *TNT*, I, p. 172.

23. C. K. Barrett, *op. cit.*, "The Hermetic Literature," pp. 80 ff.

24. Bultmann, *History and Eschatology*, p. 5.

25. Barrett, *op. cit.*, Hermes Trismegistus: "Poimandres," p. 85.

26. *PrC*, p. 163.

27. *PrC*, pp. 166 ff.; *TNT*, I, p. 174.

28. *TNT*, I, pp. 166, 174.

29. *TNT*, I, p. 167. Cf. *ST*, II, p. 44.

30. *PrC*, p. 163. Cf. Jonas, *op. cit.*, *passim*.

31. *TNT*, I, pp. 167 ff., 175–176; *PrC*, pp. 201 ff. Cf. Jonas, *op. cit.*, Ch. 2; R. Reitzenstein, *Textbuch zur Religionsgeschichte* (1922), pp. 51 ff.

32. Barrett, *op. cit.*, pp. 84 ff.; *TNT*, I, pp. 167, 176.

33. *PrC*, p. 164; *TNT*, I, p. 167.

34. *TNT*, I, pp. 169 ff.; *PrC*, p. 201.

35. *TNT*, I, pp. 178 ff.

36. *PrC*, pp. 202 f.

37. *TNT*, I, p. 180.

38. Barrett, *op. cit.*, pp. 84–87.

39. *TNT*, I, p. 164; *History and Eschatology*, pp. 54–55.

40. B. L. Woolf, *The Background and Beginning of the Gospel Story* (London: Ivor Nicholson & Watson, Ltd., 1935), p. 164.

41. According to Barrett, *op. cit.*, the Hermetic literature "gives the impression of being the deposit of many years of oral teaching," p. 80.

42. *TNT*, I, pp. 63 ff., 164 ff.

43. Bultmann, "The Approach to the Synoptic Problem," *Existence and Faith* (Meridian Books, Inc., 1960), pp. 35–55. Cf. *Die Geschichte der synoptischen Tradition*, 3d ed. (Göttingen: Vandenhoeck & Ruprecht, 1957).

44. Norman O. Brown, *op. cit.*, pp. 77 ff., 307 ff.

45. Freud, *op. cit.*, *passim;* Patrick Mullahy, *Oedipus: Myth and Complex* (Grove Press, Inc., 1955), pp. 2–65.

46. Erich Fromm, *Man for Himself* (Rinehart & Company, Inc., 1947); Mowrer, *op. cit.*, pp. 156 ff.

47. Van Deusen, *op cit.*, pp. 75 ff.

CHAPTER VIII.   Bultmann and the Ontology of Acceptance

1. Rudolf Bultmann, "New Testament and Mythology," *Kerygma and Myth,* ed. by H. W. Bartsch (London: S.P.C.K., 1957), p. 29. Cf. "The Historicity of Man and Faith," *Existence and Faith*, pp. 92 ff.; and Rudolf Bultmann, *Jesus Christ and Mythology* (Charles Scribner's Sons, 1958).

2. Oden, *Radical Obedience,* pp. 46 ff., 77 ff. Although Schubert M. Ogden has asserted that Bultmann self-contra-dictorily "both affirms and denies the ultimate identity of theology and philosophy" (*The Journal of Religion,* XXXVII, No. 3 [July, 1957], pp. 156–173), the basis upon which we defend this distinction has been set forth in "The Alleged Structural Inconsistency in Bultmann," *The Journal of Religion,* XLIV, No. 3 (July, 1964), pp. 193–200.

3. *OBP,* pp. 183–199.

4. *KM,* pp. 23–27.

5. *OBP,* pp. 199 ff.

6. *CCT, passim.*

7. *K&C,* pp. 21–26.

8. *KM,* pp. 22–33.

9. Rudolf Bultmann, *Essays* (The Macmillan Company, 1955), p. 257.

10. "The Crisis in Belief," *Essays,* pp. 2–9.

11. "The Question of Natural Revelation," *Essays,* pp. 90 ff.

12. For a fuller account of this argument, see Oden, *Radical Obedience,* pp. 57 ff.

13. Wolfhart Pannenberg, "Dogmatische Thesen zur Lehre von der Offenbarung," *op. cit.*, pp. 98–103. Cf. *Was ist der Mensch?* (Göttingen: Vandenhoeck & Ruprecht, 1962), pp. 22 ff.

14. Bultmann, *Essays,* pp. 2 ff., 95 ff. Cf. Oden, *Radical Obedience,* pp. 61–63.

15. *KM,* p. 33; this translation is found in Ogden, *op. cit.*, p. 168.

16. Fritz Buri, " Entmythologisierung oder Entkerygmatisierung der Theologie," *Kerygma und Mythos,* II (Hamburg: Herbert Reich, 1952), pp. 92 ff.; Schubert M. Ogden, *Christ Without Myth* (Harper & Brothers, 1961); Braun, *op. cit.*
17. *KM*, p. 23.
18. *KM*, p. 23.
19. *KM*, p. 24.
20. Ronald Grimsley, *Existentialist Thought* (Cardiff: University of Wales Press, 1960), pp. 35 ff., 189 ff.
21. *KM*, p. 26.
22. *KM*, p. 26.
23. *KM*, pp. 31 ff.
24. *KM*, p. 27.
25. Horney, *op. cit.*, Chs. 1–4.
26. Carl Rogers, *Psychology: A Study of a Science,* ed. by S. Koch (McGraw-Hill Book Company, Inc., 1959), pp. 205–210.
27. *KM*, p. 31.
28. Sigmund Freud, *Therapy and Technique* (Collier Books, 1963).
29. Jean-Paul Sartre, *Being and Nothingness* (Philosophical Library, Inc., 1956), ch. on " Existential Psychoanalysis."
30. *KM*, p. 30.
31. *KM*, p. 31.
32. *KM*, p. 31.

CHAPTER IX.   Worldly Theology and Psychotherapy

1. Cf. Philippe Maury, *Politics and Evangelism* (Doubleday & Company, Inc., 1959), pp. 1–51; Gayraud Wilmore, *The Secular Relevance of the Church* (The Westminster Press, 1962), pp. 1–17.
2. Arndt and Gingrich, *op. cit.*
3. Cf. Moltmann, *op. cit.*, pp. 186 ff.
4. *CD*, II/2, pp. 509 ff.
5. Cf. *The Finality of Jesus Christ in the Age of Universal History, An Ecumenical Study,* Vol. VIII, No. 2, *Bulletin,* Division of Studies, World Council of Churches, Autumn, 1962.
6. *CD*, III/4, pp. 647 ff.
7. *FJC*, pp. 11 ff.
8. André Godin, S.J., *Continuum,* Fall, 1964; cf. " L'Expérience thérapeutique du transfert et l'expérience chrétienne dans la foi," *Nouvelle Revue Théologique,* Sept.–Oct., 1965, pp. 826–831.
9. Alexander Miller, " Towards a Contemporary Doctrine of Vocation," *Christian Faith and Social Action;* John Hutchison, " The Biblical Idea of Vocation," *Christianity and Society,* Spring, 1948, pp. 9–16; E. Clinton Gardner, *Biblical Faith and Social Ethics* (Harper & Brothers, 1960), pp. 271–310; *Work and Vocation,* ed. by J. O. Nelson (Harper & Brothers, 1954).
10. Emil Brunner, *The Divine Imperative* (The Westminster

Press, 1943), pp. 198–201, 208 ff.

11. *Laity*, No. 12, Special Issue on Stewardship, Department on the Laity, World Council of Churches, 1963; Brunner, *op. cit.;* Robert Calhoun, *God and the Common Life* (Charles Scribner's Sons, 1935).

12. John Calvin, *Institutes of the Christian Religion*, I. xvi; Martin Luther, " An Appeal to the Ruling Class of German Nationality," *Martin Luther*, ed. by J. Dillenberger (Doubleday & Company, Inc., 1961), pp. 403 ff.

13. Albert C. Outler, *Psychotherapy and the Christian Message* (Harper & Brothers, 1954), pp. 43–44.

14. *Ibid.*, p. 45.

15. *Ibid.*

16. David E. Roberts, *Psychotherapy and a Christian View of Man* (Charles Scribner's Sons, 1950), p. 104.

17. *Ibid.*, p. 153.

18. Daniel Day Williams, *The Minister and the Care of Souls* (Harper & Row, Publishers, Inc., 1961), p. 11. Cf. Ch. 1, pp. 11–30.

19. *Ibid.*, pp. 25, 26.

20. *Ibid.*, p. 26 (italics mine).

21. *K&C*, Ch. IV.

22. Williams, *op. cit.*, p. 27.

23. *Ibid.*

24. *Ibid.*, p. 28.

25. Bonhoeffer, *Ethics,* pp. 55 ff.

26. Browning, *op. cit.*

27. Roberts, *op. cit.*, p. 143.

28. Karl Barth and Emil Brunner, *Natural Theology* (London: Goeffrey Bles, Centenary Press, 1946).

29. *FJC*, pp. 5 ff. This formula can without exaggeration be termed an ecumenical consensus. Cf. *FJC*, Evanston, pp. 11 ff., New Delhi, pp. 32 ff.

Epilogue

1. Ebeling, *op. cit.*, p. 360.